MAKE-IT-YOURSELF
BARRIER ACTIVITIES

by
Linda Schwartz
and
Nancy McKinley

THINKING PUBLICATIONS®
A Division of McKinley Companies, Inc.
Eau Claire, Wisconsin

07   06   05   04   03   02   01   13   12   11   10   9   8   7

ISBN 0-930599-16-0

Design and Illustrations: Robert T. Baker

Layout Composition: First Class Artistry

Printed in the United States of America

THINKING PUBLICATIONS®
A Division of McKinley Companies, Inc.

424 Galloway Street • Eau Claire, WI 54703
(715) 832-2488 • FAX (715) 832-9082
Email: custserv@ThinkingPublications.com

COMMUNICATION SOLUTIONS THAT CHANGE LIVES®

DEDICATION

To our students and our families
who continue to teach us so much about
the process we call communication

TABLE OF CONTENTS

CREDITS

The School Floor Plan on page 46 is adapted with permission from Ayres Associates (Architectural Division), Eau Claire, WI.

The maps on pages 48-50 are adapted with permission from the Seeger Map Co., Racine, WI.

The Perpetual Calendar on pages 52-54 is adapted with permission from Columbian Art Works, Inc., Milwaukee, WI. Publishers of the Perpetual® and Success® calendars. Copyright 1980.

The Auto-Touch Control Panel on page 56 is adapted with permission from Sharp Electronics Corp., Paramus, NJ.

The Base Unit of the Cordless Electronic Telephone System on page 57 is adapted with permission from Radio Shack, A Division of Tandy Corp., Fort Worth, TX.

FOREWORD

Make-It-Yourself Barrier Activities can be utilized by any professional desiring to engage children, adolescents, or adults in tasks that improve speaking, listening, and thinking skills. The resource is applicable to individuals in a wide variety of special settings such as speech-language programs, learning disabilities classrooms, and programs for the emotionally disturbed, as well as within regular classrooms. The materials are flexible enough to be used as is with students with mild to moderate impairments, to be simplified for students with severe impairments, and to be made more challenging for normal students.

Make-It-Yourself Barrier Activities should not be viewed as a rigid program, but as a resource with infinite possibilities for adaptation to individual needs. We do not believe that all students should conform to a commercial program. Conformation is inappropriate and even illegal in the sense that it does not ensure individualized educational programming as guaranteed by P.L. 94-142.

While one might be tempted to use *Make-It-Yourself Barrier Activities* without reading this accompanying guide, we ask that you resist that temptation. The guide describes the many variations possible with these materials. You will also receive valuable information derived from the literature so that you are aware of what research and theoretical constructs underpin this resource.

This resource, *Make-It-Yourself Barrier Activities*, has been adapted from *Referential Communication: Barrier Activities for Speakers and Listeners* (Parts One and Two). The original "Teachers Guide" to *Referential Communication* has been updated and reorganized for *Make-It-Yourself Barrier Activities*. Patterns from Parts One and Two are reproduced as coded line diagrams. Missing are the die-cut geometric forms needed to reconstruct patterns; users of *Make-It-Yourself Barrier Activities* are provided master forms from which they need to cut the required shapes.

We hope that you and your students enjoy using this resource as much as our students have. Above all, we hope they significantly improve their communication effectiveness as speakers and listeners as a result of participating in *Make-It-Yourself Barrier Activities*.

GOALS AND SUBGOALS OF
MAKE-IT-YOURSELF BARRIER ACTIVITIES

Goals of *Make-It-Yourself Barrier Activities*

1. To express directions and descriptions precisely, efficiently, and accurately

2. To comprehend directions and descriptions precisely, efficiently, and accurately

3. To identify when and why communication breakdowns occur

4. To repair communication breakdowns as they occur

5. To ask appropriate questions for clarification of the message

6. To assume the perspective of the communication partner(s)

7. To recognize the shared responsibility of the speaker and listener during communication

Sub-Goals of *Make-It-Yourself Barrier Activities*

1. To use planned and systematic behavior

2. To consider two or more sources of information simultaneously

3. To select relevant cues to define the problem

4. To apply comparative behavior

5. To select verbal labels and concepts that differentiate geometric forms and patterns

6. To improve spatial orientation

7. To restrain impulsive behavior

These sub-goals are based upon an analysis of the cognitive functions (Feuerstein, 1980) required within the *Make-It-Yourself Barrier Activities* tasks.

INTRODUCTION

WHAT IS REFERENTIAL COMMUNICATION?

The communication act of "informing" is known as referential communication. It requires the production and the reception of messages. The production of informative messages requires a comparison component (i.e., a speaker analyzes the stimuli to determine the attributes of the referent which distinguish it from nonreferents), a listener component (i.e., the speaker takes characteristics of the listener into account), and an evaluative component (i.e., the speaker rejects messages that would be inadequate and formulates alternatives) (Glucksberg, Krauss, and Higgins, 1975). The reception of messages requires an ability to evaluate message quality, to know that message quality affects communicative success, and to respond effectively to adequate and inadequate messages (Patterson and Kister, 1981).

During referential communication tasks, one person attempts to communicate with another person about a target referent, given a set of alternatives (Dickson and Patterson, 1981). **Referential communication tasks are commonly known as barrier activities.** Muma (1975) dubbed them "The Communication Game." During this "game," a speaker (sender) describes or explains some phenomenon to a listener (receiver) and the receiver demonstrates that the message has been received by choosing or constructing the correct referent. A barrier prevents visual stimuli from assisting the process though gestures and eye contact may be allowed. The message is conveyed by oral, gestural, and/or written channels.

To communicate referentially is to describe differences (Glucksberg, Krauss, and Higgins, 1975). Young children know how to describe differences, but do not deliberately describe them (Whitehurst and Sonnenschein, 1978). Description of differences requires comparison skills, and although young children know *how* to compare, they do not know *when* to apply comparative behavior. Whitehurst and Sonnenschein (1981) argue that comparison activity must be an accustomed skill for the child for effective referential communication (i.e., informing) to take place. Studies have shown that the tendency for speakers to give more information, after listeners give feedback that the message was inadequate, increases with age (Glucksberg and Krauss, 1967; Peterson, Danner, and Flavell, 1972). Young speakers will simply repeat their message when given general feedback about message inadequacy, while older children and adults will attempt to reformulate the message and add new information. Presumably, the ability to apply comparison skills increases with age as reflected in more adequate message sending. Ability also increases, even at young ages, when specific feedback is given. This will be discussed in a later section of this guide.

Multiple factors influence referential communication ability. Shantz (1981) summarized that "the most obvious and documented ones...[are]...the perceptual abilities to distinguish attributes of the referents and nonreferents, comparison activity of the similarities and differences between the referents and nonreferents, linguistic abilities to encode the critical differences, etc." (p. 90). **The ability of the speaker to take the perspective of the listener is also inherent within referential communication activities.**

The ability to send and to receive informative messages is assumed to be within the repertoire of any communicator and is an act repeated many times throughout a typical day. Yet engaging in precise message sending and receiving are communication skills that are not necessarily within every communicator's current abilities, particularly those individuals with language disorders, learning disabilities, or mental retardation (Feagens and Short, 1986; Monson, Greenspan, and Simeonsson, 1979; Rueda and Chan, 1980); these individuals frequently have poor referential skills or plateau at the same skill level as much younger children.

Typical referential communication activities include construction of a model, reproduction of a drawing, selection of a picture or design from an array, placement of a picture within a sequence, following directions on a map, and selecting a referent word within a list. *Make-It-Yourself Barrier Activities* emphasizes the first two activities - construction of a model and reproduction of a drawing. However, ideas for the other activities are incorporated within Appendices A and B.

The resource *Make-It-Yourself Barrier Activities* is not intended to be a static language intervention approach to be applied uniformly to all students. Rather, *Make-It-Yourself Barrier Activities* is designed to be a flexible, dynamic material, easily adaptable to meet the individual needs of a variety of students. Like all prepackaged intervention resources, there is a danger that students will be taught communication skills that do not generalize beyond the tasks presented in the publication. We might point out that this same danger can be inherent in teacher-made materials. The material, whether published or teacher-made, is not responsible for the transfer of new learning to novel situations. It is the insightful adult providing intervention services who, with every material utilized, assists students to realize that the communication skills being practiced within the structured session have far-reaching applicability in other settings.

THE THEORETICAL BASIS

Jean Piaget (1926) is credited with beginning research on children's referential communication skills. His work was extended several decades later by Flavell et al. (1968) and Krauss and Glucksberg (1969). Research on referential communication flourished in the 1970s, and several literature reviews have summarized this work (Dickson, 1981; Dickson and Moskoff, 1980). Dickson and Moskoff (1980) described characteristics of 66 publications which reported 80 experiments. From their computer-assisted analysis, they noted that most referential communication research has been conducted with normal, white, English-speaking, middle-class children. Communication performance has been related strongly to age in almost every study. Also, verbal ability has not been related strongly to communication performance except in a few studies.

Two major theoretical approaches emerge within these studies of children's referential communication ability (Asher and Wigfield, 1981): the egocentrism perspective and the task-analytic perspective. The egocentrism perspective maintains that communication failure can be attributed to the speaker's inability to take the role of the listener. Piaget (1926) observed the lack of ability that young children have to take their listener's perspective, thus making the sending of precise messages difficult during referential communication tasks. He contended that the development of communication proceeds from the egocentric speech of childhood to the socialized speech of adulthood. The task-analytic perspective "emphasizes children's difficulty in coping with the specific demands of various communication tasks" (p. 105, Asher and Wigfield, 1981). **Different communication tasks place varying demands upon speaker skills.** For example, a child may have the required vocabulary and concepts for one referential communication task, but not another.

Not surprisingly, studies have documented improved referential communication skills with increased age (Dickson and Moskoff, 1980). This developmental literature has particularly focused on children from preschool through grade five and virtually ignored the 11 to 18-year-old range. Earlier studies have adopted the egocentrism perspective to explain any communication failure (Glucksberg, Krauss, and Weisburg, 1966; Sullivan and Hunt, 1967). However, later studies have argued that communication failure results from such factors as a lack of comparison activity (Asher, 1976; Asher and Parke, 1975; Whitehurst, 1972). The argument is made that improved referential communication skills over age might be explained by an increased awareness of the need to engage in comparison activity (i.e., to compare the message with both the referent and the potential nonreferents). The improvement might also be explained by the acquisition of a more elaborate vocabulary with age. "As children's knowledge of the world increases, they would be better prepared to communicate increasingly subtle distinctions" (p. 108, Asher and Wigfield, 1981). Thus, the task-analytic perspective suggests that certain cognitive processes are relevant to successful referential communication.

The two theoretical perspectives do not need to remain mutually exclusive when it comes to training referential communication. Asher and Wigfield (1981) suggest an integration of these two perspectives, since neither one fully explains every communication failure. The current literature on normal development supports the task-analytic perspective more strongly than the egocentrism hypothesis. There is considerable evidence that young children, even those still in the pre-operational period of cognitive development, adjust their messages to the listener (Maratsos, 1973; Menig-Peterson, 1975; Shatz and Gelman, 1973). **While role-taking is not sufficient for adequate communication, it is probably a necessary factor.** However, studies have found that, even at the adolescent level, emotionally disturbed (Chandler, Greenspan, and Barenboim, 1974) and mentally retarded individuals (Longhurst, 1974) demonstrate difficulty in taking the perspective of their listeners. Emphasizing perspective-taking along with task analysis during referential communication tasks with children with disabilities appears very necessary.

In constructing *Make-It-Yourself Barrier Activities,* we have included ideas that simultaneously enhance task analysis (i.e., vocabulary/concept development and comparison behavior) and perspective taking. Thus, we have attempted to integrate both theoretical perspectives, although this resource is flexible enough to allow emphasis on one perspective over the other for the benefit of individual students.

OUR PHILOSOPHICAL PREMISES

In addition to the theoretical basis of referential communication offered by the literature, we hold certain beliefs that have influenced our development of *Make-It-Yourself-Barrier Activities*. These beliefs are shared with you in order that this resource does not become misused with students:

1. We believe that communication is the meeting of meaning between two or more people. *Make-It-Yourself-Barrier Activities* challenges participants to engage successfully in this "meeting of meaning." Language is one of the symbolic codes that permits communication to occur.

2. We believe that the "informing" function of communication is just one of several important functions to emphasize with students experiencing language disorders. **However, we recognize the informing function as one of the most necessary for academic success, and one most readily transferred from intervention sessions to other settings.**

3. We believe that deficits in referential communication have correlates with social competence (Monson, Greenspan, and Simeonsson, 1979) and academic performance, including reading (Feagens and Short, 1986).

4. We believe that communication "games" such as referential communication activities are legitimate if they meet the following criteria:

   a. They are planned with specific goals and sub-goals in mind.

   b. They are used as part of a larger curriculum, not in isolation.

   c. The strategies used to send and to receive messages are bridged to meaningful daily communication situations.

5. We believe that the message sending and receiving in referential communication activities simulate essential aspects of normal communication processes.

6. We believe that students learn from other students, not just from teachers. Therefore, we see barrier activities as very appropriate for group settings.

THE INTENDED AUDIENCE

Part One patterns of *Make-It-Yourself-Barrier Activities* are designed for children from kindergarten through grade five; Part Two patterns are designed for sixth through twelfth grade students. These divisions were derived based upon the conceptual demand of the materials. Patterns in both Parts One and Two are sequenced in order of difficulty. The adult selecting *Make-It-Yourself-Barrier Activities* should be cognizant that children with disabilities may not fit the established divison of parts, i.e., a seventh grade student with a language disorder may still be lacking vocabulary and concepts presented in Part One patterns. Several options exist: Present Part One patterns, simplify Part Two patterns, use the Item Analysis for Part One (see pages 17-18) and provide instruction for missing vocabulary and concepts.

Referential communication, or informing, is a daily activity in which communicators engage. The materials are flexible enough to be used with most disabled populations - persons with communication disorders, learning disabilities, mild to moderate hearing impairment, emotional disturbance, and mental retardation, for example. We know that many people within these special populations have impaired language and have remained concrete operational thinkers (Boyce and Larson, 1983; Larson and McKinley, 1987). But we also know that referential communication skill can be improved, even within severely mentally retarded children, when specific training is provided. For example, Biasini and Bray (1986) found that comparison training (i.e., training to compare the referent to nonreferents) and providing feedback about performance increased communication accuracy of speakers within a group of severely retarded adolescents, ages 12-14 years. Rueda and Chan (1980) determined that individuals with retardation are not "generally incompetent in referential communication, but, rather demonstrate[d] differential effectiveness depending upon the level of speakers' skill required by the task" (p. 51). *Make-It-Yourself-Barrier Activities* is a resource designed to improve the accuracy of communication and to teach higher level speaker/listener skills to participants, whether those individuals be functioning with mild, moderate, or severe deficits.

The barrier activities included in this resource provide individuals with a concrete task, yet push them toward more abstract, complex stimuli. Successful completion of the barrier activities by any student demands decentration, or the ability to assume the point of view of both the speaker and the listener, reflecting an understanding that more than one reference point possibly exists (Flavell et al., 1968). Barrier activities provide an excellent vehicle for developing increasingly higher levels of cognitive and linguistic functions using naturalistic communication. Thus, they are as appropriate for the normal population to use as for populations with disorders.

We have used barrier activities successfully down to the preschool level, but have used concrete objects as models, rather than two-dimensional drawings. The level of the drawings may be too advanced for some elementary students. If, after beginning *Make-It-Yourself-Barrier Activities*, you feel the level is too advanced, we suggest that you utilize the activities in Appendix A entitled "Readiness Barrier Activities" first.

HOW TO USE THIS RESOURCE

1. **Read this guide thoroughly.** Read through this manual before beginning the activities with your students. It will provide you with important research on referential communication and will highlight major variables to consider when planning your lessons.

2. **Establish your goals.** Determine which of the goals and sub-goals you wish to emphasize. See page viii.

3. **Select a session format and session variables.** Variations in session format (i.e., one-to-one basis or group basis) are described on pages 7-8.

   Make the activity more or less difficult by using the variables described on pages 9-12 (e.g., feedback system, questioning variations).

4. **Determine the task.** Determine whether you want the task to be one of constructing the model with cut-out forms or drawing the design illustrated on the pattern card. Strategies for encoding the message change significantly, especially within Part Two patterns of *Make-It-Yourself-Barrier Activities*, dependent upon whether the task is construction or drawing. If the task if one of construction, we suggest that listeners be supplied with the appropriate blank grid forms (see Part One and Part Two grids). If the task is one of drawing, we suggest that you use 8½"x11" white paper. You may draw in any reference lines (e.g., the line dividing the pattern card in half from top to bottom) or require the speaker to describe to the listener where to draw the reference lines. In the latter case, be certain that you have a black pen or marker available for the listener(s) to draw in the line(s).

5. **Predetermine the materials you need to assemble for the lesson.** You may make sufficient materials for any number of students to be listeners while you or another student assumes the role of speaker. However, it may not be desirable for all of the cut-out geometrical forms to be available to the student(s). You, the adult providing intervention, need to be cognizant of controlling the variables of the cut-out forms. For example, if the patterns to be used in the lesson include only red and blue forms (i.e., the referents), do you want to control for the colors red and blue and have no other colors from which to choose? If the patterns include only big forms, do you wish to include medium and small size forms from which to choose? The answers to these questions are determined by the individual needs of the student(s). However, in general we have found it desirable to control for variables when any new and unfamiliar concepts of size, shape, or color are being introduced for the first time.

6.	**Construct a barrier.**	Prevent the listener(s) from seeing the pattern to be constructed or drawn. Use a physical barrier that occludes the pattern but still allows eye contact of the communication partners (e.g., a small box, a short screen).
7.	**Determine strategies that may emerge.**	Determine probable strategies that will emerge during the referential communication activities. Plan examples of bridging the strategies and insights gained during the barrier activities to other situations in daily living. (See Appendix B for examples.)
8.	**Select a data recording system.**	Select a data recording system so that you can determine which *Make-It-Yourself-Barrier Activities* patterns have been utilized, incorporating what variables, and with what amount of communicative effectiveness. An example of a data recording system is provided in Appendix C.
9.	**Develop new patterns.**	Develop new patterns that are necessary to teach selected concepts to your students. Allow your students to design their own patterns to enhance intrinsic motivation. Don't be afraid to vary the patterns significantly from the current patterns. For example, in the patterns established by the authors, no geometrical forms overlap on the reference lines. It would certainly be possible for them to do so. It would also be feasible for you or for the students to create non-universal figures (e.g., an irregular shaped five-sided form) that the speaker must describe how to draw to the listener(s).
10.	**Allow comparisons to the master geometric form cards.**	The master geometric form cards illustrate the shapes and relative sizes of the cut-out pieces. You may wish to have the appropriate card available to students at all times as a reference. When speakers are uncertain of the sizes illustrated in the patterns, or listeners are uncertain of the size of cut-out shape to select, a comparison with the master geometric form card should establish whether the shape is big, medium, or little.

SESSION FORMAT

Referential communication has not been successful until the sender and the receiver share a common meaning for the message. Because barrier activities require both a speaker and a listener, they put communication into a very naturalistic setting, an essential component for effective language intervention (Muma, 1978). Pragmatics, or "...the ways in which normally developing children link consecutive utterance within discourse to maintain coherency and to clarify messages" (p. 106, Craig, 1983), is a primary focus throughout referential communication tasks.

Barrier activities can be successfully used on a one-to-one basis, and with small or large group settings. These variations in session format are described below.

One-to-One Basis: When using barrier activities on a one-to-one basis, care should be taken to switch the roles of sender and receiver between the student and the adult providing intervention. Between the two people should be a physical barrier or screen to prevent visual comparisons while verbal directions (oral or written) are being given. Whatever barrier is used, it should not be so high as to prevent natural eye contact. Participants may sit next to each other, across from each other, or at a ninety-degree angle. Participants may even sit back-to-back if the adult is seeking to stress the importance of nonverbal communication in message sending and receiving. However, sitting next to each other may be preferable if the activity demands left-right spatial orientation and perspective cannot yet be reversed by the student.

When in the role of sender, the adult providing intervention will usually model precise, accurate, efficient intructions. When in the role of receiver, the adult should model appropriate questions of clarification, or other feedback (see "SESSION VARIABLES" section) for the student. When communication breakdowns occur, the adult should assist the student in exploring when and why they occurred. Use of a tape recorder, especially during the initial phases of using this resource, may be advisable when giving oral directions, since frequently the student will deny what was said or not said. This problem is, of course, minimized when directions are written by the sender.

Group Basis: Four primary options exist when utilizing barrier activities in a large or small group. We are defining a small group as from two to ten students. A large group has more than ten students. While the four options described below are not the only ones, we have found them to be the most popular formats.

1. *Student Pairs:* The group can be divided into dyads and proceed with the barrier activities as described under "One-to-One Basis" above. The difference is that the adult providing intervention is now freely moving among the dyads, making relevant observations and comments, rather than interacting directly with any one student.

2. *Student Trios:* When students are divided into trios, one is designated the role of speaker, one the role of listener, and one the role of observer. This format is based upon the idea that people can more easily focus on the relation between speaker (message) and listener (response) when not enmeshed in one of those roles (Shantz, 1981). It may be that "vicarious" role reversal occurs by the observer, thus making it an effective experience.

3. *One Sender-Many Receivers:* One student can be designated as the sender while all other students in the group function as receivers or some as receivers and some as observers. If this option is chosen, the adult providing intervention must be careful to allow the students to compare their answers and to discuss communication breakdowns. Use of a tape recorder to settle disputes may be advisable, at least initially. This is less crucial if observers have been appointed. A barrier or screen is not necessary to implement this option as long as the receivers cannot see the sender's stimuli.

4. *One Receiver-Many Senders:* One student can be designated as the receiver while all other students in the group function as senders. Again, observers may be appointed, if desired. This option works better in small groups than in large groups where it is too tempting for some students to remain uninvolved. A variation of this option for larger groups is to form several smaller groups, each of which cooperatively designs the message to send to the receiver.

During implementation of any of the group options, the adult providing intervention should be sensitive to discussing the process of communication taking place, not just the end product. Many times, the activities in which the most mistakes have been made lend themselves best to analysis of the communication breakdowns. Errors should not be prevented, but rather utilized as an opportunity to discuss the pragmatics of the communication situation: When did the communication breakdown occur? Why did it occur? What question(s) could the receiver(s) have asked to clarify the message? How could repair have taken place? How did the sender (receiver) fail to take the perspective of the receiver (sender)?

Students with learning disabilities are particularly prone to making errors when in the speaker role (Knight-Arest, 1984; Feagens and Short, 1986). Knight-Arest (1984) found that, while children with learning disabilities may talk more than their nondisabled peers (i.e., they use more words and sentences), they may say less (i.e., they provide less information). When requested to clarify their messages, they often repeat rather than reformulate or increase information (Feagens and Short, 1986; Knight-Arest, 1984; Spekman, 1981). They apply fewer new strategies for overcoming communication obstacles than do their normal peers (Meline, 1985). These students, in particular, need to have their errors analyzed and alternate strategies suggested, especially those in the middle grades and older whose metalinguistic and metacognitive processes are emerging.

The adult should also ask older students (i.e., those past age ten) to bridge, or to generalize, ideas that surface during the discussion of the communication process. For example, if the students summarize the communication breakdown as occurring because of inattentiveness to relevant versus irrelevant details, ask bridging questions such as, "In what other situations is it necessary to identify relevant details? What might happen if relevant details are ignored, i.e., What are the consequences?" **Bridging is essential for students to transfer referential communication skills to other situations in school, at home, and eventually, on a job.** We cannot emphasize too much that the purpose of *Make-It-Yourself-Barrier Activities* is not simply to construct patterns of geometrical forms. Rather, the construction problems allow the adult to focus on selected goals and sub-goals of the program. (See page viii for a listing of goals and sub-goals.)

SESSION VARIABLES

Within the activities of this program, the adult providing intervention can decide whether to make the activity more or less difficult by the following variations:

1. **Communication instructions vs. perceptual instructions:** Two main types of instructions can be given to students before they begin sending informative messages: communication instructions or perceptual instructions (Whitehurst and Sonnenschein, 1981). Communication instructions tell students to describe the referent so that listeners will know the one they are describing (e.g., "Tell me about the circle in the middle of the paper so that I will know which circle you are talking about."). Perceptual instructions emphasize the description of differences (e.g., "To do a good job of playing this game, you should tell me how the circle is different."). Communication instructions may be shortened after training to "Tell me about it," and perceptual instructions may be shortened to "How is it different?" Whitehurst and Sonnenschein (1981) have found that communication instructions lead to a higher percentage of informative messages than do perceptual instructions, particularly when combined with perceptual feedback. (See the next section for information on feedback.) However, even when communication instructions are given, they are no guarantee that speaker messages will be adequate; Noel (1980) found learning disabled students were less effective in providing descriptive information about objects than non-learning disabled peers when told to generate a good description of a line drawing "so I can guess which one you are describing."

   Nonetheless, we recommend training with communication instructions rather than perceptual instructions. Communication instructions are best delivered initially by the adult providing intervention. Once modeled sufficiently, instructions, when needed, may be given by the participating students. We have found instructions to be very necessary during initial barrier activities, but may be faded as students become familiar with the tasks.

2. **Explicit feedback vs. general feedback or no feedback:** Referential communication studies have defined feedback as a reminder of a rule to contrast differences of the referent and nonreferent (Whitehurst and Sonnenschein, 1981), as a reminder of the goal of informing the listener (Whitehurst and Sonnenschein, 1981), as the task of making explicit the specific problem of the listener (Robinson, 1981), or some combination thereof. **Lack of feedback results in less informative messages than when feedback is provided.**

   Two types of feedback - communication and perceptual - have been described (Whitehurst and Sonnenschein, 1981). An example of communication feedback is, "That's right (wrong). You told me (didn't tell me) about the clown with the red feather in his hat so I knew (didn't know) which one you were talking about." An example of perceptual feedback is, "That's right (wrong). You told me (didn't tell me) how the clown with the red feather in his hat was different from the others." Of the two types of feedback, perceptual feedback leads to a higher percentage of informative messages, especially when combined with communication instructions rather than perceptual instruction. Feedback has also been labeled "confrontation" (Shantz, 1981). The speaker is confronted with the adequacy or inadequacy of the message given. Simple social feedback such as "correct - incorrect" has been found to be of little more value than no feedback at all (Whitehurst and Sonnenschein, 1981). The speaker must confront the effect(s) of the message on the listener, observe the differences between speaker's and listener's needs, and acknowledge the causal relationship between what the speaker says and what the listener does.

It may be important to keep in mind that, particularly with young children, speakers believe that they have made themselves perfectly clear and listeners believe that they have been perfectly understood (Piaget, 1926). Confrontation may facilitate decentration, believed to be a critical factor in reducing this egocentrism described by Piaget. In fact, confrontation rather than role-reversal may be more effective in training communication skills (Shantz, 1981). Simply reversing roles from speaker to listener does not make salient the relational aspect of the speaker's message and the listener's reponse. The relation is made salient through confrontation, i.e., feedback. **Listener feedback teaches speakers how to produce more adequate initial messages.** Cosgrove and Patterson (1979) have found that even 5-year-old children will produce perfect messages when the listener provides specific feedback on the exact nature of the needed information. Perceptual feedback is best modeled initially by the adult providing intervention, particularly if the other participants have language disorders. The ability of the language-disordered listener to detect the adequacy or inadequacy of the message may be quite poor at first, thus making it difficult to provide effective feedback to the speaker. For example, Kotsonis and Patterson (1980) have documented deficiencies in children with learning disabilities with regard to comprehension monitoring skills (i.e., the ability to evaluate one's level of understanding of incoming messages); children with learning disabilities had difficulty monitoring both adequate and inadequate messages. Kidder (1985) has found that even when children with learning disabilities do not understand a speaker's message, they fail to ask for clarification.

3. **Questions for clarification vs. no questions:** Initially, it is recommended that questions for clarification be allowed between the receiver and the sender. They should not only be encouraged, but modeled by the adult providing intervention. If the student's message has been too general, Robinson (1981) has found that saying, "I've got n [4, 2, or however many] like that. I'm not sure which one you mean. Can you help me?" is more effective than either saying "Which one?" or guessing which referent the speaker intends (e.g., "Is it this one?"). Saying "Which one?" is not necessarily seen by a child, particularly a young one, as an indication of message inadequacy (Robinson, 1981).

As participants become more proficient in sending and receiving messages, occasional sessions might be held during which questions for clarification are not allowed. During and after these sessions, students should discuss and bridge their experiences (e.g., How did the rule of "no questions" affect the sending and receiving of the message? Was the activity more or less difficult when questions were disallowed? What question(s) would you have asked if you could have? In what other situations have you been where you were not allowed to ask questions for clarification?).

4. **State vs. state-restate:** The usual sequence of events during barrier activities is for the sender to state the message and for the listener to demonstrate understanding. After this exchange, comparisons of the pattern being constructed are made. Another option is for the listener to restate the message to the original sender before the comparison of patterns is shared. This option will allow for identification of where misunderstanding occurred. **As listeners begin to restate what they thought senders' messages were, pinpointing of communication breakdowns is possible.** The restatement may be accomplished sequentially (i.e., as the speaker gives one part of a step-by-step direction, the listener restates all of the information).

5. **Gestures vs. no gestures:** Initially, gestures that help to clarify the spoken message may be allowed, especially for students who need the activity to be as concrete as possible. Also, gestures (e.g., pointing) are common even for adults to use when they function as an effective referential device (Pechmann and Deutsch, 1982); it would be artificial to disallow gestures totally. However, gestures which substitute for oral language (e.g., pointing to a geometric form rather than describing it) should be discouraged as soon as possible, with the exception of those students communicating by sign, so that emphasis can remain an oral communication. Pechmann and Deutsch (1982) have documented that children who cannot produce an adequate verbal description are more likely to employ nonverbal means which are inappropriate to the situation. As spatial orientation becomes an increasingly important attribute to describe, gestures might become particularly tempting. Students who did not need to use gestures initially might be instructed to rely on them heavily during one or two sessions, then to describe their actions in words. During and after these sessions, students should discuss and bridge their experiences (e.g., How did the use of gestures affect the sending and receiving of the message? Was the activity more or less difficult when gestures were allowed? In what other situations do you find it useful to use gestures?).

6. **Partial message vs. complete message:** When students begin barrier activities, it is likely that they will be more successful if partial messages are sent and received in sequential order, especially when they first encounter multiple shapes that need to be described in a particular spatial relationship to one another. After step-by-step instructions can be followed consistently, students should be required to send the entire message at once, and to receive the whole message prior to beginning the response. This requires memory strategies, thus making the level of the task more difficult. Later activities in each part of the program are specifically designed so that multiple sources of information must be considered simultaneously if the message is to be comprehended; it is impossible to continue giving sequential step-by-step instructions corresponding to step-by-step drawing or construction. This is particularly true for *Make-It-Yourself Barrier Activities*-Part Two patterns.

7. **Oral vs. written directions:** The program was designed primarily for oral language intervention. However, the sender can be instructed to write the message that the receiver then decodes (i.e., reads). For many students the use of written language will increase the difficulty of the tasks. A combination of oral and written langauge could be stressed. Students could discuss which modality is more difficult for them and why.

8. **Questions for information vs. clarification:** This variation of referential communication activities requires the listener to ask questions for information rather than questions for clarification. The speaker in turn supplies responses to these questions rather than initiating the content of the message. If "wh" questions are allowed, then question types might include, "What shapes are used?" "What colors are used?" and "Where are the shapes placed?" The activities could also be structured to require the listener to ask yes-no questions. The speaker remains in control of the pattern to be duplicated. However, the listener must employ careful questioning strategies in order to obtain all the necessary information to complete the activity successfully.

9. **Standard pattern vs. rotated pattern:** All of the patterns in *Make-It-Yourself Barrier Activities* are able to be rotated 90° left or right, or 180° upside down. Speaker messages will need to vary accordingly. The standard patterns, when used, are numbered near the upper right-hand corner of the punched edge. Patterns can be intentionally rotated when you need additional stimuli to focus on a particular concept (e.g., the standard pattern, when used, has all the forms on the *top* half, but you wish to focus on the *bottom* half so the pattern is turned 180°). The speaker can describe one pattern in four different ways by using the standard and rotated versions. Have participants bridge to other situations when different messages are given because of the different initial perspectives (e.g., a student standing at the corner of Broadway and Main Streets would give a different message for how to get to his high school than a student from the same school who is standing at the corner of Oak and Maple Streets).

Some students will want to rotate the pattern one or more times while describing it. For example, they will describe part of the pattern, rotate it and describe another part, then return to the original perspective. The adult providing intervention will need to determine whether this spontaneous rotation is permissible or not. Rotation can be a very functional strategy for speakers and, if used, should be pointed out. Bridging questions should be asked such as, ''When else is it helpful to rotate (turn) things so that we can better describe them?'' (e.g., turning a map to match our perspective; turning a three-dimensional object completely over so we can recognize what it looks like from the bottom, such as the underside of a car).

10. **Unintentional vs. intentional inadequate messages:** When first using *Make-It-Yourself Barrier Activities*, the adult providing intervention will probably want to model sending adequate messages while in the role of speaker. However, as students become familiar with what constitutes an adequate message, intentionally inadequate or ''poor'' messages can be sent by the adult. Students should have sufficient discriminative abilities to detect inadequate messages. If they do not, the students may be listener blamers, and feedback should not include counter-suggestion. (See the section entitled ''Identifying Speaker Blamers and Listener Blamers'' under ''ADDITIONAL CONSIDERATIONS.'')

When students fill the role of senders, usually there are a number of unintentional inadequate messages sent. Perceptual feedback helps to diminish these errors over time. After students are capable of consistently adequate message sending, they might be asked to intentionally send an inadequate message. The adult providing intervention may wish to work this out with the speaker before the session without the awareness of the listener(s).

ADDITIONAL CONSIDERATIONS

IDENTIFYING SPEAKER BLAMERS AND LISTENER BLAMERS

Regardless of the audience with whom *Make-It-Yourself Barrier Activities* is used, you may discover speaker blamers and listener blamers. A speaker blamer is a person who blames the speaker for communication failures, when it is appropriate to do so from the adult point of view, saying that the message was inadequate; a listener blamer is someone who blames only the listener, saying that the speaker did send an adequate message when in fact the message was inadequate (Robinson, 1981). Younger children (i.e., around 5 years old) are often listener blamers while normal 7-year-olds are often speaker blamers (Robinson and Robinson, 1976a; 1976b). Particularly when the speaker is an adult will young children cling to blaming the listener for communication breakdowns caused by inadequate messages since adult speakers are considered more intelligent and therefore, more likely to be good communicators (Sonnenschein, 1986).

Speaker and listener blamers are identified by inquiring about the reason for the communication breakdown that resulted in a failure to complete the referential communication task successfully. Correctly assigning blame for communication breakdowns "are superordinate to the child's speaking and listening evaluation and self-evaluation skills" (p. 1943, Sonnenschein and Whitehurst, 1984) and these skills transfer downward to the child's own speaking and listening. For example, children who learn to blame other speakers for ambiguous messages learn to produce fewer ambiguous messages themselves; they learn it is wrong to respond to an ambiguous message as if it were informative when in the listener role (Sonnenschein and Whitehurst, 1984).

Students who are listener blamers will find counter-suggestion by the adult (i.e., suggesting that the speaker message might have been inadequate) ineffective. For example, if an intentionally inadequate message is given by the adult, comments such as these would have absolutely no effect on message evaluation: "But you didn't know which one [picture], did you? I just said 'a flower' and you picked a flower. I didn't tell you it was the red flower." (p. 182, Robinson, 1981). Only when the adult makes explicit what the problems were in interpreting an inadequate message (e.g., too general) can listener blamers improve their own messages (e.g., "I've got four flowers. I need to know what color the flower is.") or seek clarification of another person's message.

Glucksberg, Krauss, and Higgins (1975) have summarized that there are at least three things a listener can do, when faced with an inadequate message, that would improve communication effectiveness: (1) to recognize that the message is inadequate, (2) to make this known to the speaker, and (3) to specify the additional information needed to clarify the message. Students who fail to recognize inadequate messages (i.e., they continue to blame the listener inappropriately for communication failure) may benefit from specific instruction in detecting poor messages (Flavell et al., 1981). Failure to teach recognition of inadequate messages can have severe implications for schooling. Spekman (1981) found that nine to eleven-year-old learning disabled children asked questions when faced with inadequate messages, but were less apt to use questions to gain new (i.e., not previously given) information or to acquire task-relevant, needed information; this puts them at a disadvantage when compared with their normal peer group which is capable of judging and clarifying ambiguous messages by the middle grades. As Whitehurst (1981) observed, "Indeed, it is difficult to imagine functional education in absence of children's ability to evaluate the adequacy of what they hear or read" (p. 64).

THE ROLE OF THE ADULT PROVIDING INTERVENTION

In addition to providing a role model for sending and receiving precise, accurate, and efficient messages, feedback, and questions for clarification, the adult should consider these responsibilities:

1. **Structuring the level of the program:** The two-dimensional materials designed for this resource are sequenced to become more complex and abstract. For most students, the order in which the stimuli patterns appear will correspond to a gradually increasing level of difficulty. However, exceptions may occur to which the adult should be sensitive. Do not hesitate to adjust the order of the stimuli materials, to delete patterns that are redundant for your students, or to create new patterns that are needed. The difficulty of *Make-It-Yourself Barrier Activities* will also be greatly affected by your choices made for "SESSION VARIABLES" (see pages 9-12). For example, more complex patterns can be become easier if gestures are allowed, while less complex patterns can become more difficult if questions for clarification and step-by-step directions are disallowed. For students needing simpler activities before using this program, suggestions in Appendix A, "Readiness Barrier Activities," should be applied. Some of the barrier activities described are designed for younger children and would be insulting to older students. Care should be taken, by the adult providing intervention, not to use the Readiness Barrier Activities verbatim for older children, but to extract the underlying concepts of referential communication activities which utilize concrete materials, and to adjust materials to be social-cognitive developmental level of older students.

2. **Providing precise vocabulary:** The program requires that students comprehend and express many basic labels for size, shape, color, number and spatial orientation. Adults providing intervention should be keenly aware of the vocabulary needs of their students. The item analysis charts (see pages 16-18) have organized much of this information for you. Whenever possible, the most precise label should be taught (e.g., "square," not "box"; "top right corner," not "at the top of the paper on the right side"). New vocabulary for each of the categories (e.g., size, shape) might be listed in a notebook as it is taught, to aid retention.

3. **Bridging the principles gained in the program: Bridging refers to the ability to apply principles learned in one situation to new situations.** Only when bridging successfully takes place can we expect our intervention to have a positive impact on the daily communication behavior of the student.

   A look at the goals and sub-goals listed at the beginning of this guide underlines the broad spectrum of *Make-It-Yourself Barrier Activities* and the bridging opportunities that can surface. Our concern is not that students successfully describe each stimuli pattern, but rather that they experience the essence of communication as senders and receivers. Students who are older, and have begun to acquire the ability to reflect on their language and cognitive processes, should be encouraged to analyze why communication breakdowns occurred, how they were repaired, and what might have prevented them. They should be asked to assess communication breakdowns that have occurred in other situations: Was it primarily a problem within the sender, the receiver, or both?

   Barrier activities are not just events that occur within language intervention sessions. Many common messages in daily communication involve giving and receiving precise information (e.g., "Bring my white and blue sweater that's on the floor *beside* my bed, but don't bring the blue one *on* the bed"; "Fill out Form 481-A"; "Call me at 715-876-4140"). To assist the process of applying communication strategies learned during barrier games, we have designed several "Bridging Activities" in Appendix B. These activities may be used during or after the structured pattern cards in order to emphasize the application of precise communication in daily living. They are a beginning step toward the dozens of other application activities that could be designed and would be relevent for today's youth.

ITEM ANALYSIS

An item analysis has been completed so that the progression of knowledge required by the individuals participating in *Make-It-Yourself Barrier Activities* can be seen. Each of the fifty patterns in Parts One and Two are analyzed for key concepts and vocabulary (see Tables I and II on the following pages) with the exception of Patterns 33-50 in Part Two. Concepts and vocabulary are arranged within *Make-It-Yourself Barrier Activities*-Part One patterns in developmental order as derived from normative data documented in the literature (Bangs, 1975; Boehm, 1971; Chappell, 1977; Clark, 1972; Gruenewald and Pollak, 1984; Hodun, 1975; Ilg and Ames, 1951; Johnson, 1977). There is a lack of developmental data past the primary grades. Therefore, scope and sequence charts in math and science curricula, and our personal experience in using barrier activities with language-disordered students, were used to sequence patterns from easy to difficult in Part Two patterns of this resource.

The item analysis purposely stops after Pattern 32 in Part Two because the last 18 patterns require application of previously learned concepts to solve new problems. Inspired by representational stencil design activities (Feuerstein, 1980), the last 18 patterns require a layering of geometrical forms to produce the designs illustrated. While pattern numbers 33, 34, 35, 36, 37, and 40 in Part Two can be constructed from solid color trapezoids with cut-out pieces superimposed, we would suggest that you use these items as simpler patterns from which to train layering of forms. Therefore, for Patterns 33-50 in Part Two we urge you to have *only* large trapezoid figures (solid and stencil) available to your students to use during construction tasks. We suggest that the speaker describes how to build the pattern from the bottom to the top of the design (e.g., Put the large brown trapezoid in the middle of your paper and put a red trapezoid with a tilted square cut-out on top. Put the orange trapezoid with a large circle cut-out on top of the red one.)

Part Two patterns are designed to use both big and little equilateral triangles and right isosceles triangles. The shape distinction may be too subtle for some individuals with language disorders. The two types of triangles were retained in order to provide an added challenge for participants who can benefit from it. The adult providing intervention for students who do not discriminate between equilateral and right isosceles triangles might choose one of these options: (1) control the type of triangle from which to choose (e.g., if the pattern illustrates equilateral and right isosceles triangles, present only equilateral triangles as stimuli); (2) allow physical comparison of the pattern and the cut-out triangles by the speaker (i.e., let the speaker pick up the cut-out triangles and superimpose the correct one on the pattern before formulating the message for the listener). If the speaker can discriminate between the two triangles, but the labels "equilateral" and "right isosceles" are deemed inappropriate to teach to the participants, the adult providing intervention might accept these options: (1) pointing to the correct form by the speaker in the context of the message (e.g., put this triangle [points to it] in the middle of the left half); (2) allowing description of the triangles (e.g., put the big flatter triangle [right isosceles] above the big taller triangle [equilateral]).

The relative sizes (big, medium, little) of the shapes for Part One patterns are designed to be more obvious than those for Part Two patterns. The circles in Part One, for example, are one inch (little), two inches (medium) and three inches (big) in diameter. The circles in Part Two are three-fourths of an inch, one and one-fourth inches, and one and three-fourths inches in diameter respectively for little, medium and big sizes. This is a deliberate instructional strategy to enhance increasingly subtle discrimination of sizes.

Colors of geometric forms for Part One patterns are red, blue, yellow, and green. They were chosen for their familiarity to young children even though they are not always the earliest color concepts to develop. Colors of geometric forms for Part Two patterns are red, orange, black, and brown. We felt that primary colors would be insulting to older students whereas the color scheme chosen would not be.

15

Table I Item Analysis — REFERENTIAL COMMUNICATION: Barrier Activities for Speakers and Listeners (Part One)

PATTERN NUMBER	COLOR				SIZE			SHAPE				NUMBER		POSITION							VARIABLES AND CONSTANCIES
	Red	Blue	Yellow	Green	Big	Little	Medium	Circle	Square	Triangle	Rectangle	Two	Three	Bottom	Top	Right Half/Left Half	Above/Below	Between	To the Right/Left	Size Ord./Not Size Ord.	
1	X				X			X													Size variable: shape, color constant
2	X					X		X													Size variable: shape, color constant
3	X				X			X				X									Add number (two). Size variable: shape, color constant
4	X					X		X				X									Size, number variable: shape, color constant
5	X				X			X						X							Add position (bottom). Size variable: shape, color constant
6	X					X		X							X						Add position (top). Size variable: shape, color constant
7	X				X			X							X						Size, position variable: shape, color constant
8		X			X			X							X						Add color (blue). Shape, size variable: position constant
9				X	X			X							X						Add color (green). Shape, size variable: position constant
10			X		X			X							X						Add color (yellow). Shape, size variable: position constant
11	X				X			X				X			X						Color, number variable: shape, size, position constant
12			X		X			X				X		X							Color, position, number variable: shape, size constant
13				X	X			X				X		X	X						Color, position, number variable: shape, size constant
14		X			X	X		X						X	X						Color, size, position variable: shape constant
15	X				X	X		X					X								Add number (three). Shape, color, size, position constant
16		X			X			X					X	X							Number variable: shape, color, size, position constant
17			X		X				X					X							Add shape (square). Color, size, position constant
18			X	X	X					X				X							Add shape (triangle). Color, size, position constant
19				X	X						X				X						Add shape (rectangle). Color, size, position constant
20	X			X	X	X		X		X		X		X	X						Shape, color, size, position, number variable
21	X	X		X	X	X		X		X			X			X					Add position (right half/left half). Shape, color variable: size constant
22	X		X		X	X	X	X	X							X					Add size (medium). Shape, size, position, number variable: color constant
23		X	X	X	X	X	X	X	X							X	X				Add position (above/below). Shape, color, position variable: size constant
24	X		X	X	X	X	X	X		X	X					X	X	X			Add position (between). Shape, color, size, position variable
25	X		X	X	X	X	X	X		X	X					X	X	X			Shape, color, size, position variable

16

Table I (continued)

PATTERN NUMBER	Red	Blue	Yellow	Green	Big	Little	Medium	Circle	Square	Triangle	Rectangle	Two	Three	Bottom	Top	Right Half/Left Half	Above/Below	Between	To the Right/Left	Size Ord./Not Size Ord.	VARIABLES AND CONSTANCIES
		COLOR				SIZE			SHAPE			NUMBER				POSITION					
26	X				X	X		X							X				X	X	Add position (to the right of/to the left of). Size variable. shape. color constant
27			X	X	X	X		X						X					X	X	Color. size. position variable. shape constant
28			X	X	X	X			X					X					X		Shape. size. position variable. color constant
29	X	X	X		X	X		X	X	X				X	X				X		Shape. color. size. position variable
30	X	X		X	X	X		X	X	X				X	X				X		Shape. color. size. position variable
31	X			X	X	X				X	X				X			X	X		Color. size. position variable. shape constant
32	X	X	X	X	X	X			X	X				X	X			X	X		Color. size. position variable. shape constant
33	X	X	X	X	X			X				X		X	X				X		Shape. color. size. position. number variable
34	X	X					X	X			X					X			X		Shape. position variable. color. size constant
35	X					X	X		X					X	X	X			X		Color. size variable. shape. position constant
36			X	X	X	X		X					X	X	X			X	X		Color. size. position. number variable. shape constant
37	X	X	X	X		X	X							X	X			X	X		Color. size variable. shape constant
38	X	X	X	X		X	X		X	X	X					X		X	X		Shape. color. position variable. size constant
39	X	X	X	X	X	X	X		X	X	X					X		X	X		Shape. color. size. position variable
40	X	X	X	X	X	X	X	X								X	X	X	X		Shape. color. size. position variable
41			X	X	X	X	X	X						X	X			X	X		Color. position variable. shape constant
42		X	X	X	X	X	X	X						X				X	X	X	Add position (size order). Size variable. shape. color constant
43			X	X	X	X	X		X	X				X	X			X	X	X	Add position (not size order). Size variable. shape. color constant
44	X	X	X	X	X	X	X	X	X	X	X			X	X			X	X	X	Shape. color. size. position variable
45	X	X	X	X	X	X	X	X			X			X	X			X	X	X	Shape. color. size. position variable
46	X	X	X	X	X	X	X	X										X	X		Color. size variable. shape constant
47	X	X	X	X	X	X	X	X	X	X	X			X		X		X	X		Shape. color. size. position variable
48	X	X	X	X	X	X	X		X	X				X	X		X	X	X	X	(Grid removed) Color. size. position variable. shape constant
49	X	X	X	X	X	X	X	X	X	X	X			X	X			X	X		Shape. color. size. position variable
50	X	X	X	X		X	X		X	X	X				X	X	X	X	X	X	Shape. color. size. position variable

17

Table II Item Analysis — REFERENTIAL COMMUNICATION: Barrier Activities for Speakers and Listeners (Part Two)

Pattern Number	Left of Left Half	Right of Right Half	Horizontal	Vertical	Size Order	Size Differentiation	Shape Differentiation	Above/Below	Diagonal (on a diag.)	Not size order	Upper/Rt., Lower/Lt.	On top of/On	Joined	Equal in Size	Thirds (Rt., Lt., Middle)	Middle, Center, Centered, Midpoint	Thirds (Upper, Lower, Middle)	Between	Parallel	Apex	Base	Fourths Quarters	Overlap	Semi-Circle	Clockwise/Counterclockwise
1	X	X	X	X		X								X											
2	X	X			X	X	X	X																	
3	X	X	X	X		X	X	X																	
4	X	X				X	X																		
5	X	X		X		X	X											X							
6	X	X	X		X	X	X		X	X	X	X	X												
7	X	X	X			X					X		X												
8	X	X	X	X	X	X	X				X														
9						X		X			X														
10	X	X				X			X		X	X		X				X							
11			X	X		X	X	X	X						X										
12			X			X	X	X							X										
13	X	X	X	X	X	X	X	X	X		X	X	X	X		X	X	X	X	X	X				
14	X	X	X			X	X						X	X		X	X			X					
15						X	X	X								X									
16	X	X	X	X		X	X				X	X	X	X	X	X	X		X	X	X	X	X		
17	X	X	X			X	X	X	X		X	X	X		X	X	X		X	X	X		X	X	X
18	X	X	X	X		X		X			X		X	X	X	X	X	X		X	X	X			X
19			X	X		X		X							X	X	X							X	
20			X	X		X	X	X	X		X	X	X	X	X	X	X		X					X	
21				X								X	X	X		X									
22				X	X								X	X		X		X					X		
23													X			X									
24	X	X	X			X	X	X	X		X	X	X	X		X									
25	X	X	X		X	X		X								X									
26	X	X			X	X										X									
27				X		X	X	X	X		X	X		X	X	X	X		X	X	X				X
28	X		X	X		X	X	X				X				X				X		X			X
29			X			X			X													X	X		
30	X	X		X		X	X	X	X		X	X	X	X						X	X				
31	X	X	X			X	X	X			X	X	X	X		X				X	X		X	X	
32	X	X	X			X	X	X			X	X	X	X		X							X	X	

18

Spatial orientation of the shapes becomes an increasingly important variable in the speaker's message for both Part One and Part Two patterns. Initially, the adult providing intervention may wish to consider spatial orientation as irrelevent. For example, Pattern Number 1 in Part One illustrates a big red circle in the middle of a blank grid. It would be advisable for some children initially to eliminate the demand of describing orientation of the form in favor of emphasizing size, shape, and/or color variables.

Part Two patterns occasionally illustrate diagonal, horizontal, and vertical black lines drawn on the geometric forms. You may choose to direct your students to ignore these lines while constructing the patterns from geometric forms. (Note: The lines were included primarily for use during drawing tasks.) If you want to have the lines described during construction tasks, mark the necessary geometric forms with lines using a black grease pen. Speakers will still need to describe these lines in their messages for listeners to select the correct form (e.g., Use the big brown square with a line. The line should be in the middle and vertical.). The lines can remain permanently affixed; assuming your forms are reversible, they can be turned to the unlined side whenever desired. Black lines marked directly on your grids can be wiped off if you laminate the grids before using them.

RECORD KEEPING

Because of the versatility of this resource, we suggest that data be maintained throughout the use of these materials. We have developed a specific form for this purpose. The implication is not that you would use *Make-It-Yourself Barrier Activities* in isolation during intervention, but rather, when you do, that you would maintain accurate records. To facilitate this process, we have developed a data recording sheet. It may also substitute for the lesson plan, or at least supplement it. The form can be found in Appendix C and duplicated.

BIBLIOGRAPHY

Asher, S. Children's ability to appraise their own and another person's communication performance. *Developmental Psychology.* 12:24-32, 1976.

Asher, S. and Parke, R. Influence of sampling and comparison processes on the development of communication effectiveness. *Journal of Educational Psychology.* 67:64-75, 1975.

Asher, S. and Wigfield, A. Training referential communication skills. In W. Dickson (ed.), *Children's Oral Communication Skills.* New York: Academic Press, 1981.

Bangs, T. *Vocabulary Comprehension Scale: Pronouns and Words of Position, Size, Quality and Quantity (Scoring Form).* Austin, TX: Learning Concepts, 1975.

Biasini, F. and Bray, N. Comparison and message-formulation skills in the referential communication of severely mentally retarded children. *American Journal of Mental Deficiency.* 90 (6):686-693, 1986.

Boehm, A. *Boehm Test of Basic Concepts Manual.* New York: The Psychological Corporation, 1971.

Boyce, N. and Larson, V. *Adolescents' Communication: Development and Disorders.* Eau Claire, WI: Thinking Publications, 1983.

Chandler, M., Greenspan, S. and Barenboim, C. Assessment and training of role-taking and referential communication skills in institutionalized emotionally disturbed children. *Developmental Psychology.* 10:546-553, 1974.

Chappell, G. A cognitive-linguistic intervention program: Basic concept formation level. *Language, Speech and Hearing Services in Schools.* 8:23-32, 1977.

Clark, E. On the child's acquisition of antonyms in two semantic fields. *Journal of Verbal Learning and Verbal Behavior.* 11 (6):750-758, 1972.

Cosgrove, J. and Patterson, C. Adequacy of young speakers' encoding in response to listener feedback. *Psychological Reports.* 45:15-18, 1979.

Craig, H. Applications of pragmatic language models for intervention. In T. Gallagher and C. Prutting (eds.), *Pragmatic Assessment and Intervention Issues in Language.* San Diego, CA: College-Hill Press, 1983.

Dickson, W. (ed.) *Children's Oral Communication Skills.* New York: Academic Press, 1981.

Dickson, W. and Moskoff, M. *A Meta-analysis of Referential Communication Studies: A Computer Readable Literature Review* (Theoretical Paper No. 83). Madison, WI: Wisconsin Research and Development Center for Individualized Schooling, UW-Madison, May 1980.

Dickson, W. and Patterson, J. Evaluating referential communication games for teaching speaking and listening skills. *Communication Education.* 30 (1):11-21, 1981.

Feagans, L. and Short, E. Referential communication and reading performance in learning disabled children over a 3-year period. *Developmental Psychology.* 22 (2):177-183, 1986.

Feuerstein, R. *Instrumental Enrichment.* Chicago, IL: Scott, Foresman, 1980.

Flavell, J., Botkin, P., Fry, C., Jr., Wright, J. and Jarvis, P. *The Development of Role-taking and Communication Skills in Children.* New York: Wiley and Sons, 1968.

Flavell, J., Speer, J., Green, F. and August, D.   The development of comprehension monitoring and knowledge about communication. *Monographs of the Society for Research in Child Development.* 46 (5, Serial No. 192); 1981.

Glucksberg, S. and Krauss, R.   What do people say after they have learned to talk? Studies of the development of referential communication. *Merrill-Palmer Quarterly.* 13:309-316, 1967.

Glucksberg, S., Krauss, R. and Higgins, E.   The development of referential communication skills. In F. Horowitz (ed.), *Review of Child Development Research (Vol. 4).* Chicago: University of Chicago Press, 1975.

Glucksberg, S., Krauss, R. and Weisberg, R.   Referential communication in nursery school children: Method and some preliminary findings. *Journal of Experimental Child Psychology.* 3:333-342, 1966.

Gruenewald, L. and Pollak, S.   *Language Interaction in Teaching and Learning.* Austin, TX: Pro-Ed, 1984.

Hodun, A.   *Comprehension and the development of spatial and temporal sequence terms.* Unpublished doctoral dissertation, University of Wis.-Madison, 1975.

Ilg, F. and Ames, L.   Developmental trends in arithmetic. *Pedagogical Seminary and Journal of Genetic Psychology.* 79:3-28, 1951.

Johnson, E. G.   The development of color knowledge in preschool children. *Child Development.* 48 (1):308-311, 1977.

Kidder, J.   *Requesting clarification: The neglected aspect of listening.* Paper presented at the Conference of the Association of Children and Adults with Learning Disabilities. San Francisco, CA, Feb. 20-23, 1985.

Knight-Arest, I.   Communicative effectiveness of learning disabled and normally achieving 10-to-13-year-old boys. *Learning Disability Quarterly.* 7:237-245, 1984.

Kotsonis, M. and Patterson, C.   *Comprehension monitoring in learning disabled and normal children.* Paper presented at the Biennial Southeastern Conference on Human Development. Alexandria, VA, April 17-19, 1980.

Krauss, R. and Glucksberg, S.   The development of communication: Competence as a function of age. *Child Development.* 40:255-266, 1969.

Larson, V. and McKinley, N.   *Communication Assessment and Intervention Strategies for Adolescents.* Eau Claire, WI: Thinking Publications, 1987.

Longhurst, T.   Communication in retarded adolescents: Sex and intelligence level. *American Journal of Mental Deficiency.* 78 (5):607-618, 1974.

Maratsos, M.   Nonegocentric communication skills in preschool children. *Child Development.* 44:697-701, 1973.

Meline, T.   *Verbal strategies by specific language impaired.* Paper presented at the Annual Convention of the American Speech-Hearing-Language Association. Washington, DC, Nov. 22-25, 1985.

Menig-Peterson, C.   The modification of communication behavior in preschool-aged children as a function of the listener's perspective. *Child Development.* 46:1015-1018, 1975.

Monson, L., Greenspan, S. and Simeonsson, R.   Correlates of social competance in retarded children. *American Journal of Mental Deficiency,* 83 (6):627-630, 1979.

Muma, J.   *Language Handbook: Concepts, Assessment, Intervention.* Englewood Cliffs, NJ: Prentice-Hall, 1978.

Muma, J.   The communication game: Dump and play. *Journal of Speech and Hearing Disorders.* 40:296-309, 1975.

Noel, M.   Referential communication abilities of learning disabled children. *Learning Disability Quarterly.* 3:70-75, 1980.

Patterson, C. and Kister, M.   The development of listener skills for referential communication. In W. Dickson (ed.), *Children's Oral Communication Skills.* New York: Academic Press, 1981.

Pechmann, T. and Deutsch, W.   The development of verbal and nonverbal devices for reference. *Journal of Experimental Child Psychology.* 34:330-341, 1982.

Peterson, C., Danner, F. and Flavell, J.   Developmental changes in children's responses to three indications of communicative failure. *Child Development.* 43:1463-1468, 1972.

Piaget, J.   *Language and Thought of the Child.* New York: Harcourt, Brace, 1926.

Robinson, E.   The child's understanding of inadequate messages and communication failure: A problem of ignorance or egocentrism? In W. Dickson (ed.), *Children's Oral Communication Skills.* New York: Academic Press, 1981.

Robinson, E. and Robinson, W.   Developmental changes in the child's explanation of communication failure. *Australian Journal of Psychology.* 28:155-165, 1976a.

Robinson, E. and Robinson, W.   The young child's understanding of communication. *Developmental Psychology.* 12:328-333, 1976b.

Rueda, R. and Chan, K.   Referential communication skill levels of moderately mentally retarded adolescents. *American Journal of Mental Deficiency.* 85 (1):45-52, 1980.

Shantz, C.   The role of role-taking in children's referential communication. In W. Dickson (ed.), *Children's Oral Communication Skills.* New York: Academic Press, 1981.

Shatz, M. and Gelman, R.   The development of communication skills: Modifications in the speech of young children as a function of listener. *Monographs of the Society for Research in Child Development.* 38 (5, Serial No. 152), 1973.

Sonnenschein, S.   Development of referential communication: Deciding that a message is uninformative. *Developmental Psychology.* 22 (2):164-168, 1986.

Sonnenschein, S. and Whitehurst, G.   Developing referential communication: A hierarchy of skills. *Child Development.* 55 (5):1936-1945, 1984.

Spekman, N.   Dyadic verbal communication abilities of learning disabled and normally achieving fourth-and fifth-grade boys. *Learning Disability Quarterly.* 4:139-151, 1981.

Sullivan, E. and Hunt, D.   Interpersonal and objective decentering as function of age and social class. *Journal of Genetic Psychology.* 110:199-210, 1967.

Whitehurst, G.   Commentary. *Monographs of the Society for Research in Child Development.* 46 (5, Serial No. 192), 1981.

Whitehurst, G.   The development of communication: Changes with age and modeling. *Child Development.* 47:473-482, 1972.

Whitehurst, G. and Sonnenschein, S.   The development of informative messages in referential communication: Knowing when versus knowing how. In W. Dickson (ed.), *Children's Oral Communication Skills.* New York: Academic Press, 1981.

Whitehurst, G. and Sonnenschein, S.   The development of communication: Attribute variation leads to contrast failure. *Journal of Experimental Child Psychology.* 25:454-490, 1978.

Appendix A
READINESS BARRIER ACTIVITIES

Readiness Barrier Activities

If the level of abstraction of activities developed for *Make-It-Yourself Barrier Activities* proves too high, it is suggested that some or all of the concrete activities described within this appendix section be completed first. Relevant information for all barrier activities presented in this resource should be utilized in these readiness tasks.

I. OBJECT MANIPULATION

Materials needed: Screen, identical duplicate set of manipulable objects (e.g., cup, comb, book, magazine, etc.)

Activity: The screen is placed between the speaker and the receiver. The speaker instructs the receiver which objects should be selected and the spatial relationship they should have to one another. Initially only two or three items might be used, whereas later many could be. The screen could be used as the referent point for concepts like "near" and "far," although the screen can also remain an entirely neutral barrier.

Sample Messages: On top of the magazine put the book. Under the magazine put the comb.

Put the magazine in between the comb and the book. The book should be on top.

Select three objects - two that we can read from and one from which we drink. Put the one from which we drink in the middle, with the things we read on either side. The one with the most pages should go on the right side.

(Note: The complexity of the language can be changed by using descriptions instead of object labels, or by using association [e.g., put the object that goes with _____ next to . . .], function [e.g., put the object you use to _____ next to . . .], and analytic perception [e.g., put the object with the _____ part next to . . .]. Possibilities are endless. Language can be simplified to begin, and gradually become more complex.)

II. BLOCK PATTERNS - FREE DESIGN

Materials needed: Screen, identical set of blocks (may vary in color and/or shape and/or size, if desired)

Activity: The screen is placed between the speaker and the listener. The speaker instructs the receiver which blocks should be selected and the spatial relationship they should have to one another. Initially only two or three items might be used, whereas later many could be. The task can be made increasingly complex by adding additional variables of size, shape, and color. One variable at a time can be added, while controlling for others, if the activities need to be gradually made more difficult for the student.

Sample Messages: Put three blocks in a row. Put a fourth block on top of the middle block (variables of size, shape, color all controlled, i.e., all blocks are identical).

Build a tower of five blocks. Put two red blocks on the bottom, then a yellow block in the middle, and two blue blocks on top (color as a variable; size and shape controlled).

Make a square with four large blocks. Put a small block on the middle of the square (size as a variable; color and shape controlled).

Make a horizontal row of five blocks. Put two rectangular blocks on either end of the row and a triangular block in the middle (shape as a variable; color and size controlled).

Make a vertical column of four blocks. The top of the column should be a big red block, below that should be two small blue blocks, and a medium green block should be on the bottom (size and color as variable; shape controlled).

Build a triangle with three red rectangular blocks. Put a blue square block inside the triangle (color and shape as variables; size controlled).

Put three blocks on top of each other. A large rectangular block should be the base, followed by a medium square block, and then a small triangular block (size and shape as variables; color controlled).

Make a row of three blocks. On the left place a big red rectangular block, in the middle put a small red square block, and on the right put a medium-size blue triangular block (color, size, and shape as variables).

III. BLOCK PATTERNS - CONTROLLED DESIGN

Materials: Screen, prepared block patterns (commercially purchased or teacher-made)

Activity: The screen is placed between the speaker and the listener. Using a prepared block pattern, the sender instructs the receiver how to construct the pattern in three-dimensional space using blocks that conform to the pattern variables. As with the preceding Readiness Barrier Activity, size, shape, and color variables can be systematically controlled and altered.

Sample Messages: Build two towers of three blocks each side-by-side. The tower on the left should have a red block on the botton, then a blue block, then a yellow block. The tower on the right should have a black block on the bottom, then a green block, then a red block. The two towers should be touching each other.

IV. PEG PATTERNS

Materials: Screen, pegs and pegboards, prepared pegboard patterns (optional) (Note: For younger children use larger plastic pegs; for older students use smaller pegs suitable to their social developmental level.)

Activity: The screen is placed between the speaker and the listener. Both participants have pegs and a pegboard. If patterns are being used, the speaker has the pattern and the receiver has the pegboard and pegs. The speaker instructs the receiver how many pegs to select, and where to put them on the board, using specific spatial referents (e.g., third row, fourth hole from the left side). As with other manipulable items, the number can initially be small and then gradually expanded. Color may be held constant or become a dynamic variable in this activity.

Sample Messages: Put a peg in the top left corner, the bottom right corner, and in the third row, second hole from the left. (Color is controlled by having all pegs an identical color.)

Place a green peg in the top row, fourth hole from the left and a blue peg in the sixth row, third hole from the right side.

Place two yellow pegs in the middle of the top row and two orange pegs in the middle of the right-hand side of the board.

V. GIFT WRAP GUESS

Materials: Screen, two pieces of identical gift wrap with a multitude of illustrated characters and activities (Two identical action pictures or posters could be substituted.)

Activity: The screen is placed between the speaker and the listener. Each participant has an identical piece of gift wrap. The speaker instructs the listener to find specific details within the illustration and to indicate comprehension by marking the detail in some way. (If the gift wrap is to be reused for future barrier activities, care should be taken not to mark the paper with a marker.)

Sample Messages: Put a block on the hat of the boy who has red hair and freckles and put a block on the flower next to the girl who is blowing out the birthday candles.

Put an "x" on the shoes of the girl who is pulling the wagon and color the bow on the biggest teddy bear red.

Put number 1 on the blue flower in the top right corner, number 2 on the apron of the girl in the middle of the picture, and number 3 on the tail of the puppy next to her. (Small cutout numbers are used.)

VI. NUMBER - LETTER BARRIERS

Materials: Screen, identical pages that contain the letters of the alphabet and/or numbers. (Use a range suitable to the developmental level of the student.)

Activity: The screen is placed between the speaker and the listener. Each participant has an identical page of numbers and/or letters. The speaker instructs the receiver to mark specific numbers and/or letters. In order to make the activity more concept orientated, and less memory orientated, the speaker could be instructed not to mention the desired number or letter by name (e.g., rather than saying, "Put an 'x' on number 12," say "Put an 'x' on the number of months in a year.").

Sample Messages: Put an "x" on the letter your name starts with, put a circle around the letter your brother's name starts with, and put a square around the letter that is last in the word 'cat.' (letters only).

Put a red block on the number of seconds in a minute and a blue block on the number of days in a week (numbers only).

Put a line under the letters in the word "Stop," put a circle around the vowels, and put a square around all the odd numbers (numbers and letters).

VII. IDENTICAL CHARACTERS

Materials: Screen, identical people except for slight variations in dress and facial expression (see following pages)

Activity: The screen is placed between the speaker and the listener. Both participants have identical illustrations of people in front of them. Variations include:

1. Present only one illustration. Messages to color various items of clothing can be sent.

2. Present several or all of the illustrations on one page. Messages to color different items of clothing on a variety of people can be sent.

3. Have the illustrations colored before the session begins. The speaker selects one of the people as the referent and describes it so that the listener can select it from the nonreferents. At first, the referent and nonreferents can be colored to share few attributes, while later they can share many.

(Note: Simplify the illustrations as needed for your students. For example, cut off the hat on a figure. This will become a very obvious difference to describe. You can also add additional attributes. For example, trace the illustrations and give some people striped shirts, rather than striped pants.)

Sample Messages: Color the stripes green and the hat blue (illustration of only one person given).

Color the narrow stripes on the sleepy person yellow and the short hat on the happy person with the narrow stripes blue (illustration of several or all people given).

I'm thinking of the person who has a happy look, a short red hat, and narrow orange stripes on his pants (illustration of several or all people given).

34

35

VIII. WORD LISTS

Materials: Screen, identical word pairs or word lists

Activity: The screen is placed between the speaker and the listener. Use the paired word lists that follow on the next page or create similar ones. Each participant should have identical words. The word pairs may be printed on index cards if the task needs to be simplified. A third and fourth word may be added to the pair to make the task more difficult. The speaker determines which word is the referent and describes the word without using the word itself. Make certain that the sender and receiver understand the universe of words from which to choose (e.g., if the entire word list of six pairs of words is presented, make certain both participants know that the first referent being described is one of the two words at the top of the list).

Sample Messages: Choose the word that is an animal. (car - dog)

I'm thinking of the color that is the color of the sky on a nice day. (red - blue)

This is a leader of a country who wears a crown. He's a man. (president - king)

car - dog
flower - milk
book - light
window - door
house - tree
bread - butter

paper - pencil
sheet - blanket
red - blue
branch - leaf
meat - vegetable
moon - star

boy - girl
adult - baby
white - black
heavy - light
love - hate
lake - ocean

June - July
east - north
summer - spring
mother - father
Wednesday - Tuesday
right - left

president - king
pen - marker
thin - skinny
wife - mother
junk - garbage
fence - enclosure

dream - fantasy
ugly - mean
enjoyment - fun
expensive - rich
smart - clever
peace - justice

37

IX. PICTURES IN A SEQUENCE

Materials: Screen, identical sets of teacher-made or commercial story sequence cards

Activity: The screen is placed between the speaker and the listener. Each participant has a set of story sequence cards. The sender describes to the listener the order in which to place the cards. You may require the traditional sequential order dictated by the story cards, or allow the students to disregard the story and to describe a random sequence of pictures. If random sequence is allowed, any identical set of pictures would work for stimuli, since the story line has become irrelevant.

Sample Messages: First the boy gets out of bed, then he brushes his teeth (boy is still in pajamas), then he gets dressed. (Traditional sequence order is followed.)

Put the picture of the boy brushing his teeth first, then the picture of him getting dressed, then the picture of him getting out of bed. (Order of pictures is relevant to the description provided, but not to the traditional temporal sequential expectations.)

X. REFERENT-NONREFERENT CLUES

Materials: Screen, identical set of geometrical forms for *Make-It-Yourself Barrier Activities*.

Activity: The screen is placed between the speaker and the listener. Place the predetermined, identical set of geometrical forms in front of both participants. At first a small controlled number of forms can be used; later a larger number of forms can be selected as adequate message sending improves. Have the sender describe one of the forms (the referent) so that the listener can determine the referent from the nonreferent. The speaker may take responsibility for selecting the referent, or the adult providing intervention can indicate to the sender which referent to describe.

Sample Messages: It's big and it's red. (Only big and little circles in assorted colors have been given to the participants. Since no other shapes are available from which to choose, the mentioning of "circle" in the message, while acceptable, is irrelevant.)

It's a green square. (Only big forms in assorted colors and shapes have been given to the participants. Therefore, it is irrelevant to include a description of size in the message.)

I'm thinking of a medium blue triangle. (Forms in assorted colors, shapes, and sizes have been given to the participants. Therefore, it is necessary to include all attributes of color, shape, and size in the message.)

It's the little green rectangle to the right of the big blue circle. (Several identical forms are included in the set of items given to the participants. Now spatial orientation becomes relevant to identify the referent.)

Appendix B
BRIDGING ACTIVITIES

Bridging Activities

We recommend that you ask questions which promote bridging throughout the use of *Make-It-Yourself Barrier Activities*. This will occur by asking questions such as "In what other situations have you used that concept (strategy, word)? When have you found it important to give clear messages? Name other times when a communication breakdown has occurred and why?"

Five bridging activities are included in this manual. They are not intended to be exhaustive of the common situations in which referential communication occurs, but rather to provide a sampling of natural contexts and to encourage students to become aware of when precise messages must be expressed and comprehended. The bridging activities included in this section include sample messages and reproducible materials.

I. STORAGE CLOSET

Sample Messages: Go to the closet and get the catsup on the top shelf and the container marked "Flour."

Go to the closet and get the broom. Check to see if the mop is there, too.

(Note: Items in the closet may be colored if it is desirable to add the dimension of color. "Getting" an item can be indicated by putting a token on the named item, or by some other agreed upon means.)

II. SCHOOL FLOOR PLAN

Sample Messages: If I told you to start in the assistant principal's office, turn left, go down the hall, turn right, and go three doors down on your left, what room would you be in?

From the "Commons" area, take the northeast exit, turn right, go down to the first intersection, turn left and go three doors down on your right. What room is that?

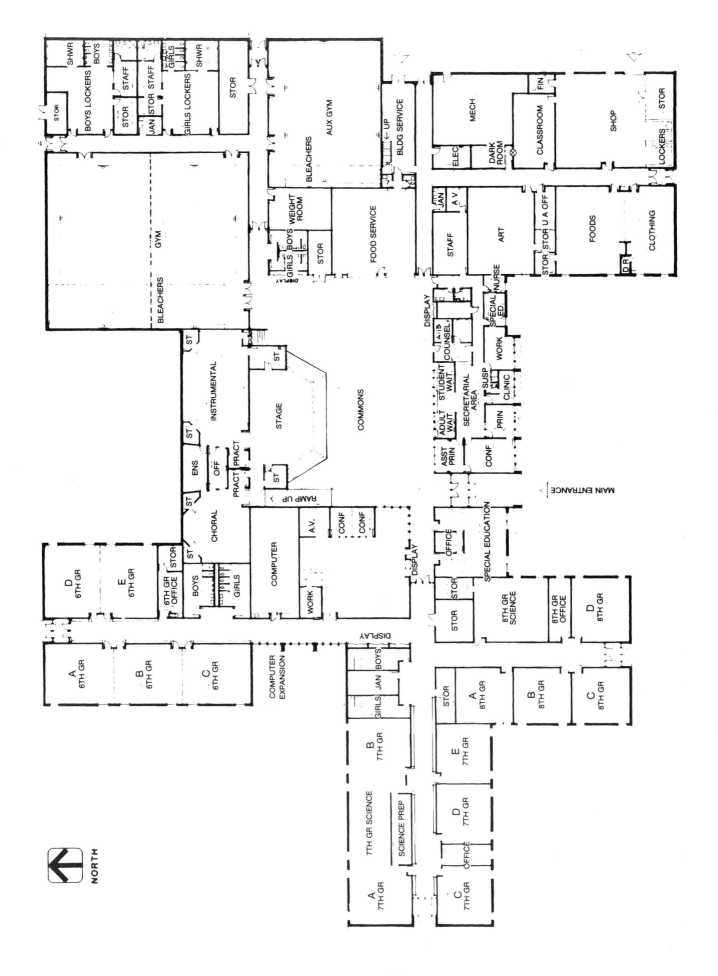

46

III. MAPS

Sample Messages: Beginning at Washington School, go toward the City Hall on Lincoln Avenue. Turn right on Park Avenue and go until you reach Franklin Street.

From Evergreen Park take Shorewood Drive to North 2nd Avenue East. Turn left. Go to 17th Street East.

Take Highway 12 from County Hospital Road west to Highway 25. Turn left and go to 20th Avenue East. Turn right and I'll meet you at the corner of 20th Avenue and 3rd Street West.

(Note: Many identical maps can be used, from very simple ones to complex ones. City, regional, state, or country maps might be used. The maps on the next pages are examples of the possibilities that exist.)

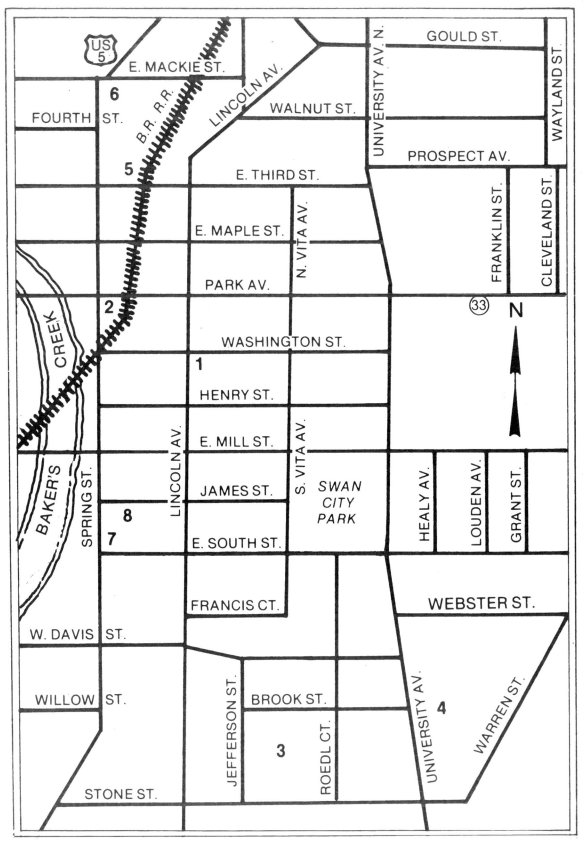

1. City Hall
2. Free Library
3. Washington School
4. Community Hospital
5. Fire Hall #2
6. United States Post Office
7. Central High School
8. Middle School

LAKE MENOMIN

EVERGREEN PARK

POINT COMFORT RD

24TH ST. E

NORTH CT

N 7TH AVE.

AURORA CIR

21ST ST. E.

24TH ST. E.

SHOREWOOD DR.

N 6TH AVE. E

N 4TH AVE. E.

N. 3RD ST. E

AVE. E.

STOUT R'

N. 2ND AVE. E

SERVICE RD E

1ST AVE. E.

17TH ST. E

18TH ST. E.

19TH ST. E

2ND AVE. E

2ND ST. E.

3RD AVE. E.

LAKEVIEW PK

3RD AVE. E.

14TH ST. E.

15TH

16TH

22ND ST. E.

5TH AVE. E.

5TH AVE. E.

16TH ST. E

6TH AVE. E.

15TH ST. E

16TH ST. E

DUNN CO. FAIR ASSOC.

MAIN ST.

11TH ST. E

12TH ST. E

13TH ST. E

15TH ST. E

OAKWOOD ST. E

OAKWOOD BLVD

16TH

15TH

10TH ST. E.

12TH ST. E

N↑

49

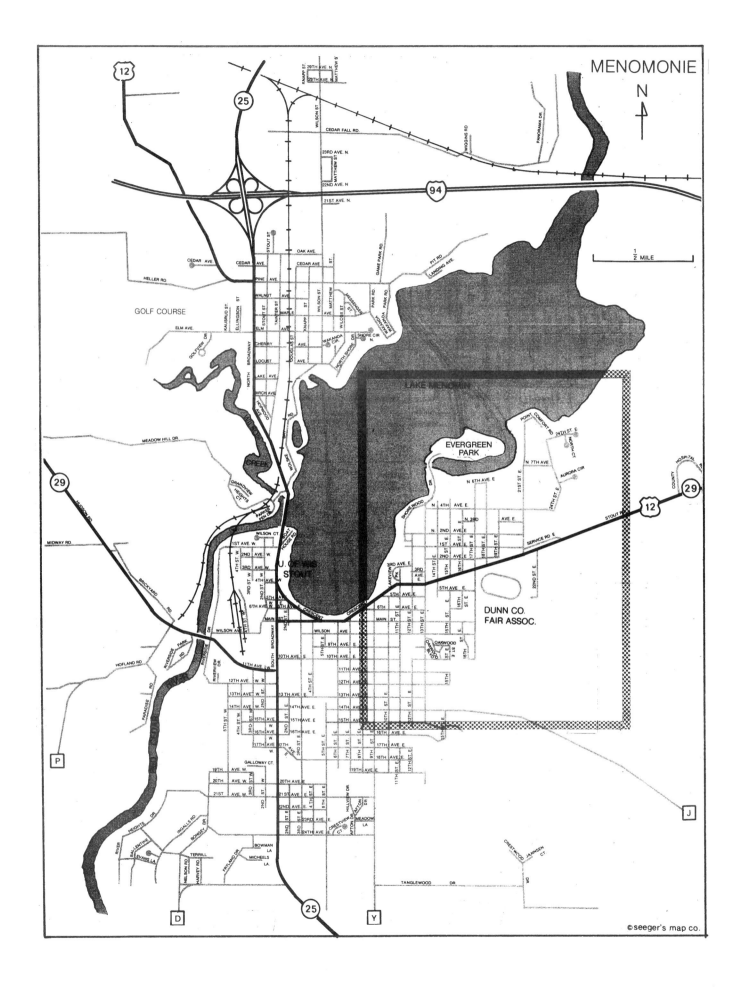

MENOMONIE

N

GOLF COURSE

LAKE MENOMIN

EVERGREEN
PARK

U. OF WIS
STOUT

DUNN CO.
FAIR ASSOC.

©seeger's map co.

IV. PERPETUAL CALENDAR

Sample Messages: Find what day of the week Halloween will be this year, and the Fourth of July next year.

Tell me what day of the week your birthday was in 1890, and what day it will be next year.

INSTRUCTIONS FOR THE USE OF THE PERPETUAL CALENDAR ON THE FOLLOWING PAGES

Pick the desired year from the preceding tables of years 1700-2108. Opposite the desired year is a letter. Turn to the lettered calendars which follow the tables. Use the calendar which has the same letter as that opposite the desired year in the tables.

EXAMPLE — July 4, 1776. Turn to the tables and find the year 1776. Opposite 1776 is the letter J. Turn to calendar J and you find that our Declaration of Independence was adopted by the Continental Congress in Philadelphia on Thursday, July 4, 1776.

1700 - 1799

Yr	L	Yr	L	Yr	L	Yr	L
1700	H	1729	A	1757	H	1785	A
1701	I	1730	H	1758	I	1786	H
1702	D	1731	I	1759	D	1787	I
1703	E	1732	D	1760	E	1788	D
1704	M	1733	E	1761	M	1789	E
1705	B	1734	M	1762	B	1790	M
1706	H	1735	B	1763	H	1791	B
1707	I	1736	H	1764	I	1792	H
1708	L	1737	I	1765	L	1793	I
1709	F	1738	L	1766	F	1794	L
1710	A	1739	F	1767	A	1795	F
1711	C	1740	A	1768	C	1796	A
1712	D	1741	B	1769	D	1797	B
1713	E	1742	C	1770	E	1798	C
1714	B	1743	D	1771	B	1799	D
1715	C	1744	E	1772	C		
1716	D	1745	G	1773	D		
1717	D	1746	H	1774	D		
1718	J	1747	I	1775	J		
1719	A	1748	D	1776	A		
1720	B	1749	J	1777	B		
1721	H	1750	A	1778	H		
1722	K	1751	B	1779	K		
1723	E	1752	H	1780	E		
1724	F	1753	K	1781	F		
1725	A	1754	E	1782	A		
1726	N	1755	F	1783	N		
1727	I	1756	A	1784	I		
1728	D						

1800 - 1899

Yr	L	Yr	L	Yr	L	Yr	L
1800	A	1829	A	1857	A	1885	A
1801	H	1830	H	1858	H	1886	B
1802	I	1831	I	1859	I	1887	H
1803	D	1832	D	1860	D	1888	I
1804	E	1833	E	1861	E	1889	L
1805	M	1834	M	1862	M	1890	F
1806	B	1835	B	1863	B	1891	A
1807	H	1836	H	1864	H	1892	B
1808	I	1837	I	1865	I	1893	C
1809	L	1838	L	1866	L	1894	D
1810	F	1839	F	1867	F	1895	E
1811	A	1840	A	1868	A	1896	G
1812	B	1841	B	1869	B	1897	H
1813	C	1842	C	1870	C	1898	I
1814	D	1843	D	1871	D	1899	D
1815	E	1844	E	1872	E		
1816	G	1845	G	1873	G		
1817	H	1846	H	1874	H		
1818	I	1847	I	1875	I		
1819	D	1848	D	1876	D		
1820	J	1849	J	1877	J		
1821	A	1850	A	1878	A		
1822	B	1851	B	1879	B		
1823	H	1852	H	1880	H		
1824	K	1853	K	1881	K		
1825	E	1854	E	1882	E		
1826	F	1855	F	1883	F		
1827	A	1856	A	1884	A		
1828	N						

1900 - 2012

Yr	L	Yr	L	Yr	L	Yr	L
1900	E	1929	E	1957	E	1985	E
1901	F	1930	F	1958	F	1986	A
1902	A	1931	A	1959	A	1987	B
1903	B	1932	B	1960	B	1988	H
1904	C	1933	C	1961	C	1989	K
1905	D	1934	D	1962	D	1990	E
1906	E	1935	E	1963	E	1991	F
1907	F	1936	F	1964	F	1992	A
1908	G	1937	G	1965	G	1993	N
1909	H	1938	H	1966	H	1994	I
1910	I	1939	I	1967	I	1995	D
1911	D	1940	D	1968	D	1996	E
1912	J	1941	J	1969	J	1997	M
1913	A	1942	A	1970	A	1998	B
1914	B	1943	B	1971	B	1999	H
1915	H	1944	H	1972	H	2000	I
1916	K	1945	K	1973	K	2001	L
1917	E	1946	E	1974	E	2002	F
1918	F	1947	F	1975	F	2003	A
1919	A	1948	A	1976	A	2004	B
1920	N	1949	N	1977	N	2005	C
1921	I	1950	I	1978	I	2006	D
1922	D	1951	D	1979	D	2007	E
1923	E	1952	E	1980	E	2008	G
1924	M	1953	M	1981	M	2009	H
1925	B	1954	B	1982	B	2010	I
1926	H	1955	H	1983	H	2011	D
1927	I	1956	I	1984	I	2012	L
1928	L						

2013 - 2108

Yr	L	Yr	L	Yr	L	Yr	L
2013	E	2041	E	2069	E	2097	E
2014	F	2042	F	2070	F	2098	F
2015	A	2043	A	2071	A	2099	A
2016	B	2044	B	2072	B		
2017	C	2045	C	2073	C		
2018	D	2046	D	2074	D		
2019	E	2047	E	2075	E		
2020	F	2048	F	2076	F	2100	G
2021	G	2049	G	2077	G		
2022	H	2050	H	2078	H		
2023	I	2051	I	2079	I		
2024	D	2052	D	2080	D		
2025	J	2053	J	2081	J		
2026	A	2054	A	2082	A		
2027	B	2055	B	2083	B		
2028	H	2056	H	2084	H		
2029	K	2057	K	2085	K		
2030	E	2058	E	2086	E		
2031	F	2059	F	2087	F		
2032	A	2060	A	2088	A		
2033	N	2061	N	2089	N		
2034	I	2062	I	2090	I		
2035	D	2063	D	2091	D		
2036	E	2064	E	2092	E		
2037	M	2065	M	2093	M		
2038	B	2066	B	2094	B		
2039	H	2067	H	2095	H		
2040	I	2068	I	2096	I		

PICK DESIRED YEAR FROM ABOVE. LETTER INDICATES WHAT CALENDAR TO USE FOR THAT YEAR.

A 1986

```
      JAN                      FEB                      MAR
S  M  T  W  T  F  S                     1                        1
         1  2  3  4      2  3  4  5  6  7  8      2  3  4  5  6  7  8
5  6  7  8  9 10 11      9 10 11 12 13 14 15      9 10 11 12 13 14 15
12 13 14 15 16 17 18    16 17 18 19 20 21 22    16 17 18 19 20 21 22
19 20 21 22 23 24 25    23 24 25 26 27 28       23 24 25 26 27 28 29
26 27 28 29 30 31                              30 31

      APR                      MAY                      JUNE
      1  2  3  4  5                  1  2  3    1  2  3  4  5  6  7
6  7  8  9 10 11 12      4  5  6  7  8  9 10     8  9 10 11 12 13 14
13 14 15 16 17 18 19    11 12 13 14 15 16 17    15 16 17 18 19 20 21
20 21 22 23 24 25 26    18 19 20 21 22 23 24    22 23 24 25 26 27 28
27 28 29 30             25 26 27 28 29 30 31    29 30

      JULY                     AUG                      SEPT
      1  2  3  4  5                     1  2       1  2  3  4  5  6
6  7  8  9 10 11 12      3  4  5  6  7  8  9     7  8  9 10 11 12 13
13 14 15 16 17 18 19    10 11 12 13 14 15 16    14 15 16 17 18 19 20
20 21 22 23 24 25 26    17 18 19 20 21 22 23    21 22 23 24 25 26 27
27 28 29 30 31          24 25 26 27 28 29 30    28 29 30
                        31

      OCT                      NOV                      DEC
         1  2  3  4                        1       1  2  3  4  5  6
5  6  7  8  9 10 11     2  3  4  5  6  7  8     7  8  9 10 11 12 13
12 13 14 15 16 17 18    9 10 11 12 13 14 15    14 15 16 17 18 19 20
19 20 21 22 23 24 25   16 17 18 19 20 21 22    21 22 23 24 25 26 27
26 27 28 29 30 31      23 24 25 26 27 28 29    28 29 30 31
                       30
```

B 1987

```
      JAN                      FEB                      MAR
S  M  T  W  T  F  S     1  2  3  4  5  6  7     1  2  3  4  5  6  7
            1  2  3     8  9 10 11 12 13 14     8  9 10 11 12 13 14
4  5  6  7  8  9 10    15 16 17 18 19 20 21    15 16 17 18 19 20 21
11 12 13 14 15 16 17   22 23 24 25 26 27 28    22 23 24 25 26 27 28
18 19 20 21 22 23 24                           29 30 31
25 26 27 28 29 30 31

      APR                      MAY                      JUNE
         1  2  3  4                     1  2       1  2  3  4  5  6
5  6  7  8  9 10 11     3  4  5  6  7  8  9     7  8  9 10 11 12 13
12 13 14 15 16 17 18   10 11 12 13 14 15 16    14 15 16 17 18 19 20
19 20 21 22 23 24 25   17 18 19 20 21 22 23    21 22 23 24 25 26 27
26 27 28 29 30         24 25 26 27 28 29 30    28 29 30
                       31

      JULY                     AUG                      SEPT
         1  2  3  4                        1          1  2  3  4  5
5  6  7  8  9 10 11     2  3  4  5  6  7  8     6  7  8  9 10 11 12
12 13 14 15 16 17 18    9 10 11 12 13 14 15    13 14 15 16 17 18 19
19 20 21 22 23 24 25   16 17 18 19 20 21 22    20 21 22 23 24 25 26
26 27 28 29 30 31      23 24 25 26 27 28 29    27 28 29 30
                       30 31

      OCT                      NOV                      DEC
                  1     1  2  3  4  5  6  7          1  2  3  4  5
4  5  6  7  8  9 10     8  9 10 11 12 13 14     6  7  8  9 10 11 12
11 12 13 14 15 16 17   15 16 17 18 19 20 21    13 14 15 16 17 18 19
18 19 20 21 22 23 24   22 23 24 25 26 27 28    20 21 22 23 24 25 26
25 26 27 28 29 30 31   29 30                   27 28 29 30 31
```

F 1991

G 1992

H 1993

C 1988

D 1989

E 1990

I 1994

J

K

L

M

N

V. MECHANICAL DIRECTIONS

Sample Messages: Press "Convection," then "375° F," then "Cook."

Find the "Code Enter" button, then the Telephone Connection Cable.

(Note: Touching the picture in the correct sequence would be an acceptable response format.)

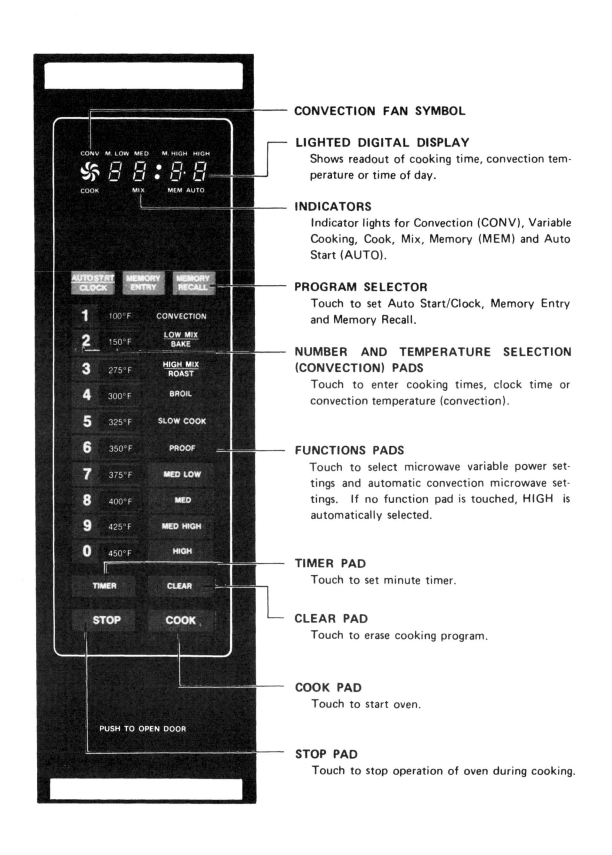

CONVECTION FAN SYMBOL

LIGHTED DIGITAL DISPLAY
Shows readout of cooking time, convection temperature or time of day.

INDICATORS
Indicator lights for Convection (CONV), Variable Cooking, Cook, Mix, Memory (MEM) and Auto Start (AUTO).

PROGRAM SELECTOR
Touch to set Auto Start/Clock, Memory Entry and Memory Recall.

NUMBER AND TEMPERATURE SELECTION (CONVECTION) PADS
Touch to enter cooking times, clock time or convection temperature (convection).

FUNCTIONS PADS
Touch to select microwave variable power settings and automatic convection microwave settings. If no function pad is touched, HIGH is automatically selected.

TIMER PAD
Touch to set minute timer.

CLEAR PAD
Touch to erase cooking program.

COOK PAD
Touch to start oven.

STOP PAD
Touch to stop operation of oven during cooking.

BASE UNIT

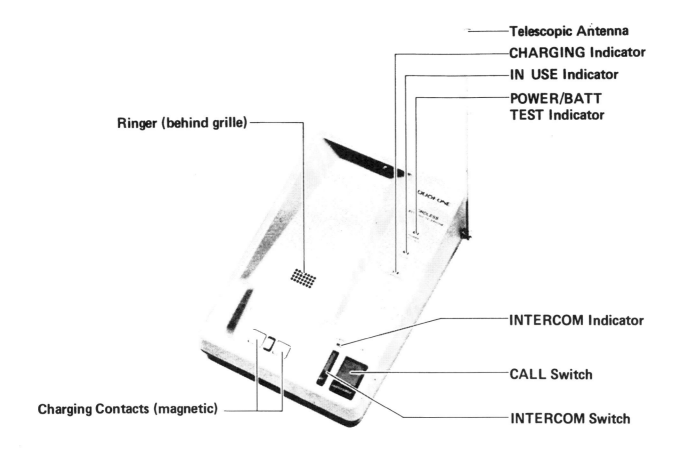

Ringer (behind grille)

Telescopic Antenna

CHARGING Indicator

IN USE Indicator

POWER/BATT TEST Indicator

INTERCOM Indicator

CALL Switch

INTERCOM Switch

Charging Contacts (magnetic)

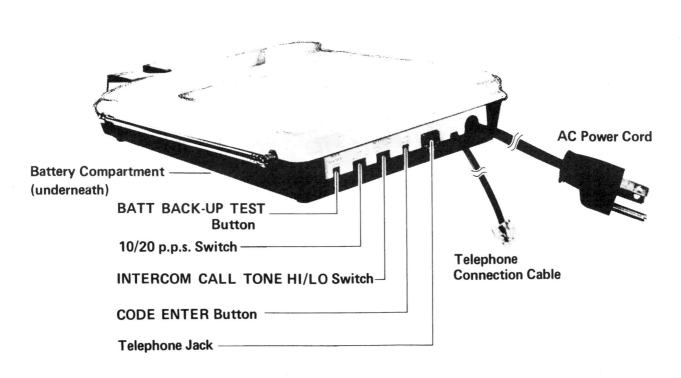

AC Power Cord

Battery Compartment (underneath)

BATT BACK-UP TEST Button

10/20 p.p.s. Switch

INTERCOM CALL TONE HI/LO Switch

CODE ENTER Button

Telephone Jack

Telephone Connection Cable

Appendix C
DATA RECORDING FORM

Make-It-Yourself Barrier Activities
Nancy McKinley and Linda Schwartz

Date: _____

Student: _____
or
Group: _____

DATA RECORDING FORM

Session Format
____ One-to-One   ____ One Speaker, Multiple Listeners
____ Student Pair   ____ One Listener, Multiple Speakers
____ Student Trio   ____ Other _____

Barrier Activity
____ Model Construction
____ Drawing of Design
____ Other _____

Part I   ____ Pattern Card(s): _____
Part II   ____ Standard
          ____ Rotated _____ °
          ____ Self-Generated Patterns
               (see attached)

Session Variables

No   Yes
____ ____ 1. Instructions given
____ ____ 2. Feedback given
____ ____ 3. Questions for clarification
____ ____ 4. State-restate required
____ ____ 5. Gestures allowed
____ ____ 6. Partial (sequential) message
____ ____ 7. Simultaneous message
____ ____ 8. Oral directions
____ ____ 9. Written directions
____ ____ 10. Questions for information

Concepts/Vocabulary to Emphasize

Goals/Sub-Goals to Emphasize

Strategies That May Emerge

Bridging Ideas

COMMUNICATION EFFECTIVENESS

____ No. of adequate messages
____ No. of inadequate messages

STUDENT OR GROUP PERFORMANCE NOTES

Thinking Publications®, A Division of McKinley Companies, Inc.

© 1985, 1987

61

Appendix D
CONSTRUCTING *MAKE-IT-YOURSELF BARRIER ACTIVITIES*

Preparing for Construction

In preparation for constructing *Make-It-Yourself Barrier Activities*, you may find it useful to gather the following materials:

water-based color markers or colored pencils
Part One: red, blue, green, yellow
Part Two: orange, brown, red, black

black marker, preferably fine-tip felt, for outlining geometrical forms on pattern cards

scissors

medium-weight white or colored tag board

Optional:

plastic bags with locking tops for storing cut-out geometrical forms

carrying case or storage unit for materials (preferably one which could also act as the barrier between the listener and the speaker)

clear contact paper or lamination for protecting pattern plates

carbon paper for tracing geometrical forms

tissue paper for tracing geometrical forms

Using the Coded Line Diagrams

The plates contained in this resource have diagrams with coded lines for your ease in constructing the barrier activities. The codes illustrated on the next page should be adhered to when coloring the plates so that the progression of knowledge required of the student corresponds to the item analysis on pages 16 through 18. We recommend copying the plates and coloring the copies, allowing you to use the originals many times when additional patterns are needed.

We recommend using water-based color markers when coloring the plates since permanent markers tend to bleed over a period of time. We also recommend that once you color the geometrical patterns, you outline the forms using a fine-tip black marker, thus covering the coded lines. If you decide to color the patterns directly in this resource, without duplicating them first, we recommend you use colored pencils.

Constructing the Manipulative Geometrical Forms

Using the Geometric Form Masters, trace the geometrical figures onto tag board or heavy-weight paper and cut out. Use these cut-out forms as patterns for tracing and cutting more forms.

One strategy for making this task simpler might be to place the Geometric Form Masters upon the carbon paper which is placed on the tag board (carbon toward the tag board). Tracing the outline of the form will transfer the form to the tag board.

One could also use tissue paper to trace the forms from the master card. Use the tissue paper, layered upon the carbon paper and tag board and again trace the tissue paper forms, thereby transferring them to the tag board.

Using the patterns for various geometrical forms, trace and cut enough forms of each color for the number of listeners who will need them. Most of the time, to complete a pattern plate, no more than two of each shape of a particular size and color will be needed (e.g., two large green circles, two medium-size green circles, etc.). However, in Part One, you will need three small red circles, three large blue circles, and three large yellow circles for each listener. Rarely in Part Two do you need three of any geometrical form; the exception is plate number 31 which requires three small black circles.

PART ONE

RED	————————————
YELLOW	- - - - - - - - -
GREEN	—·—·—·—·—
BLUE	— — — — —

PART TWO

RED	- - - - - - - - -
BLACK	— ·· — ·· — ·· —
ORANGE	—··—··—··—
BROWN	— — — — —

WHITE or NO COLOR (black line only) ———————————

EXAMPLES:

Part One:

green   red   yellow   blue

Part Two:

red   brown   orange

orange   red   brown   red   red   orange

66

The patterns can be traced onto colored tag board or white tag board which would then have to be colored before cutting out. Whichever technique is used, the colors of the manipulative geometrical forms should be consistent with the colors of the geometrical forms on the plates.

If you find it will be distracting to your students not to have the black line borders outlining these geometrical forms as the pattern plates do, add them when constructing the shapes.

Part Two, plates 33-50, require stenciled trapezoids. Using the Geometric Form Masters found in this resource, again create patterns of the trapezoid stencils, cutting out the middle superimposed form (e.g., a trapezoid with a small circle cut out from the middle). Using these patterns, create the four different colored trapezoid stencils (orange, black, brown, red) required for use in plates 33-50.

Materials to Gather Before Using Your Barrier Activities

Other materials you may find useful to have available when using the barrier activities are the following:

Part One

Red, blue, green and yellow markers (1 set for each listener)

Black pen or fine-tip marker (1 for each listener)

Blank paper (8½"x11")

Part Two

Red, orange, brown, and black markers (1 set for each listener)

Black pen or fine-tip marker (1 for each listener)

Blank paper (8½"x11")

Black grease pens (1 for each listener)

Part One Patterns

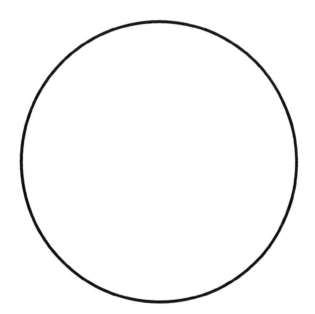

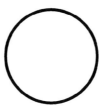

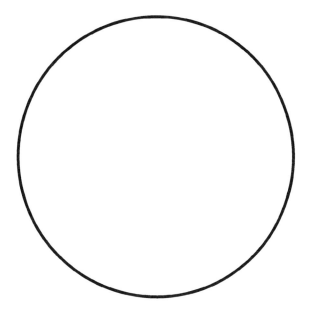

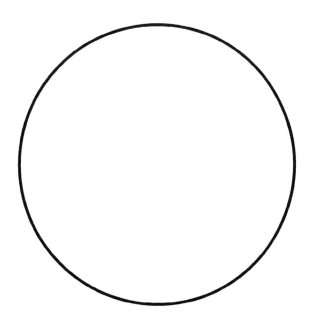

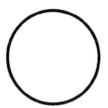

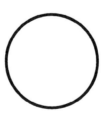

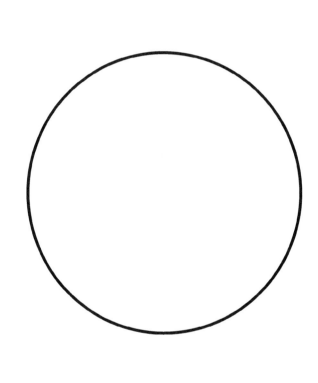

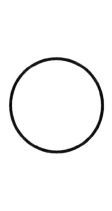

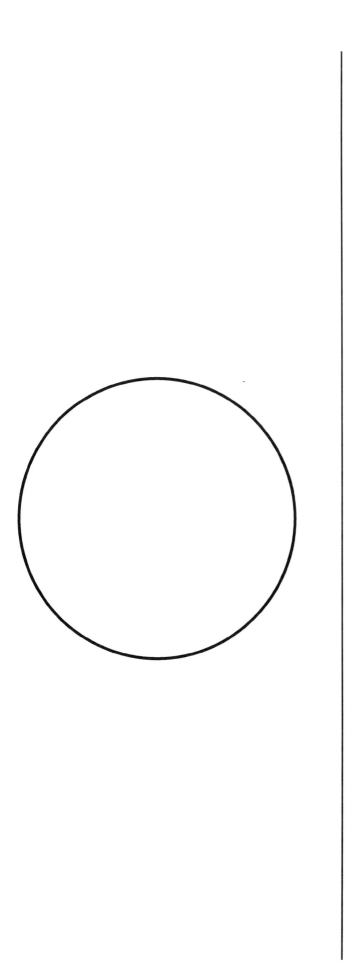

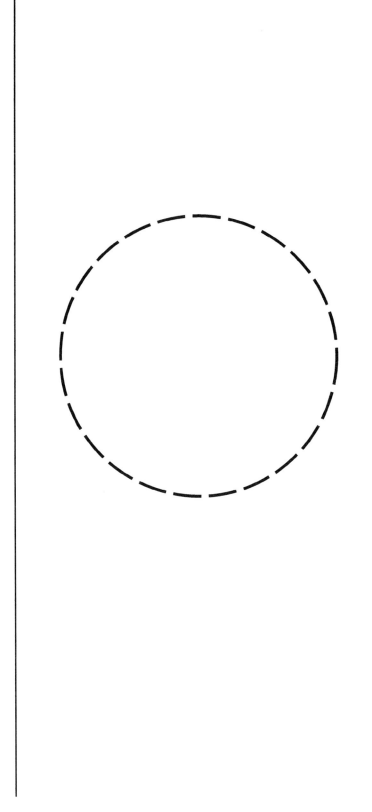

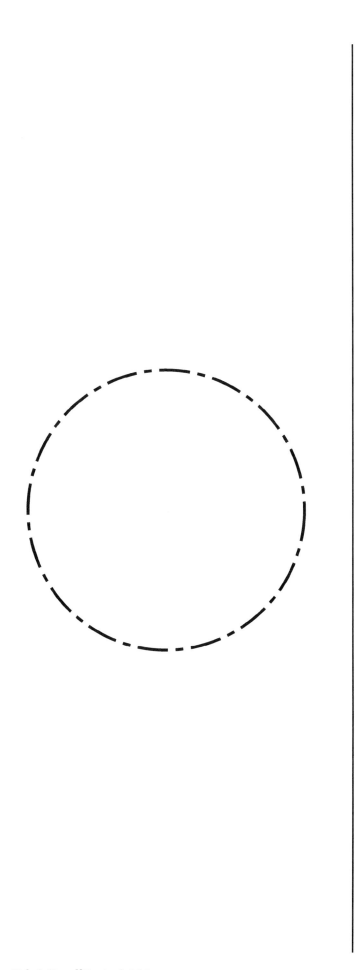

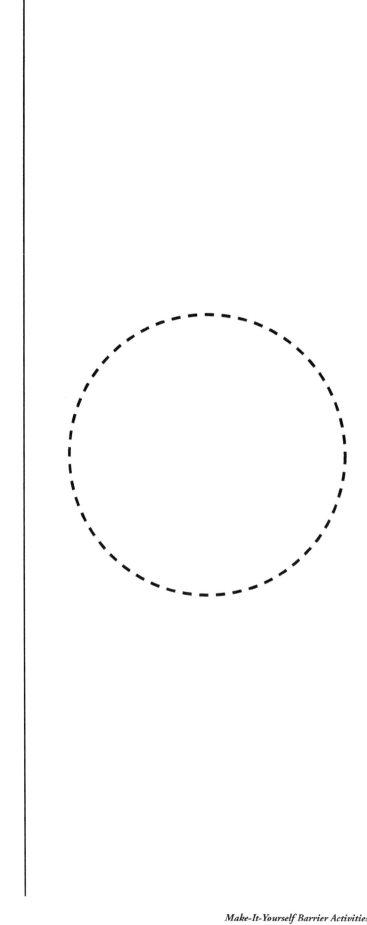

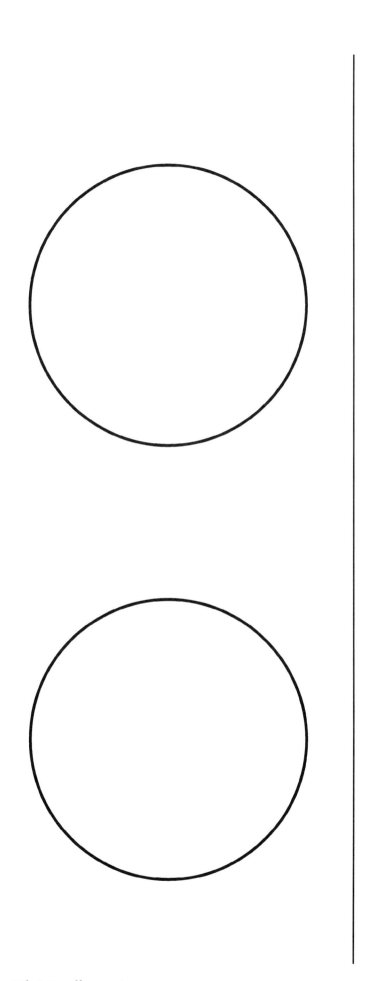

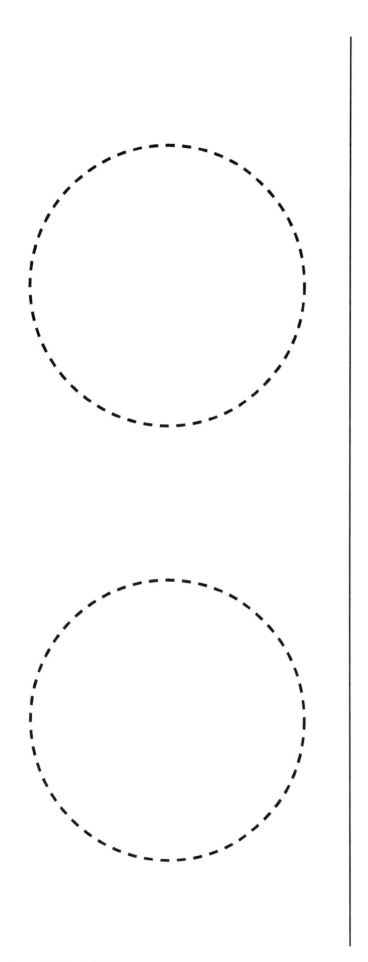

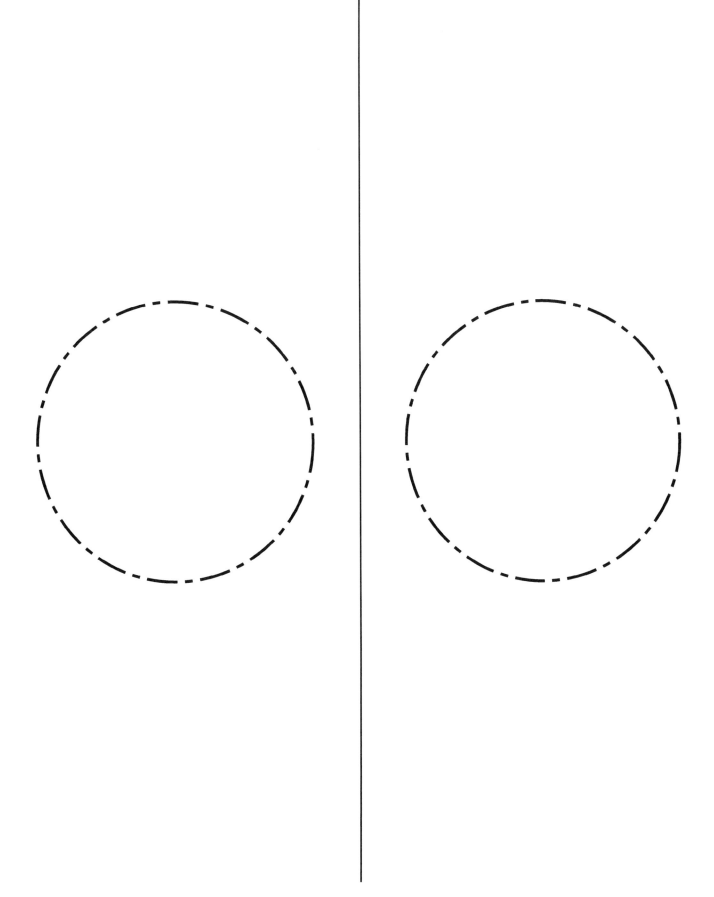

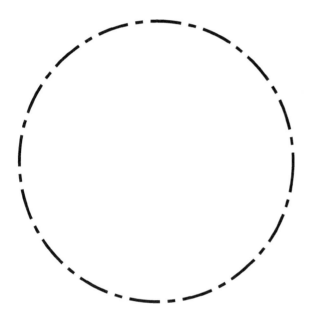

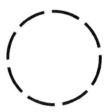

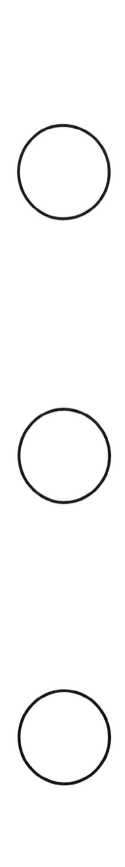

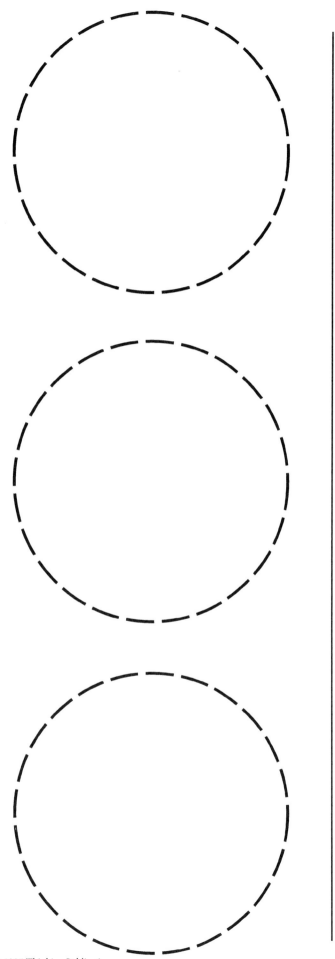

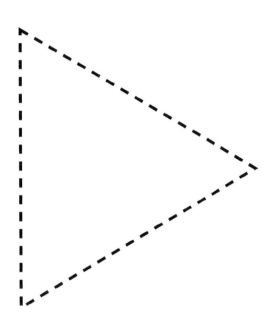

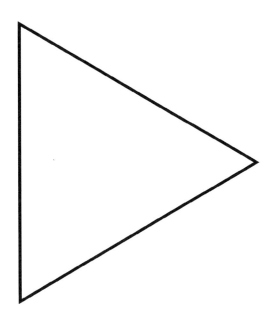

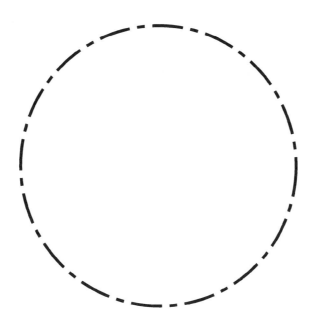

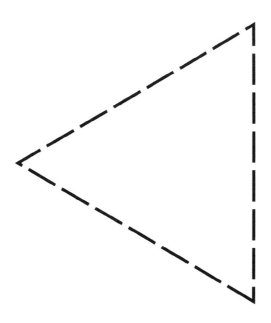

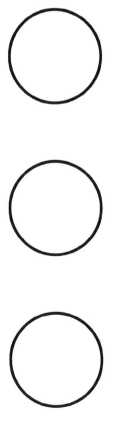

 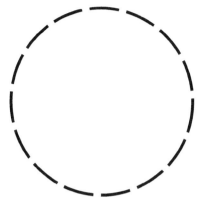

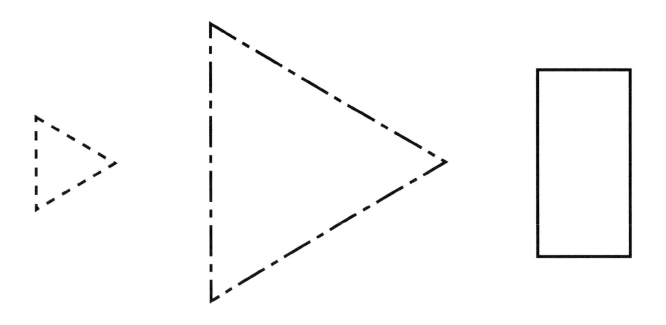

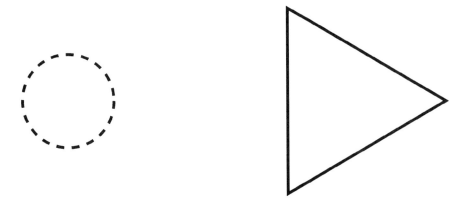

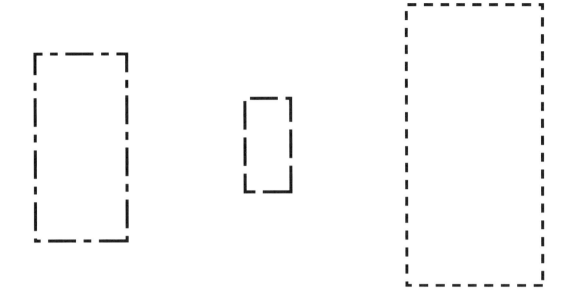

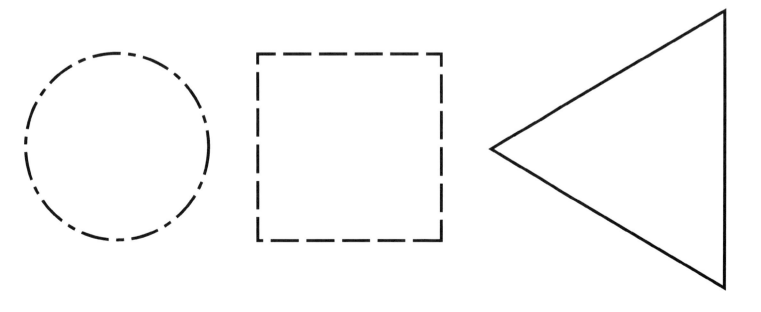

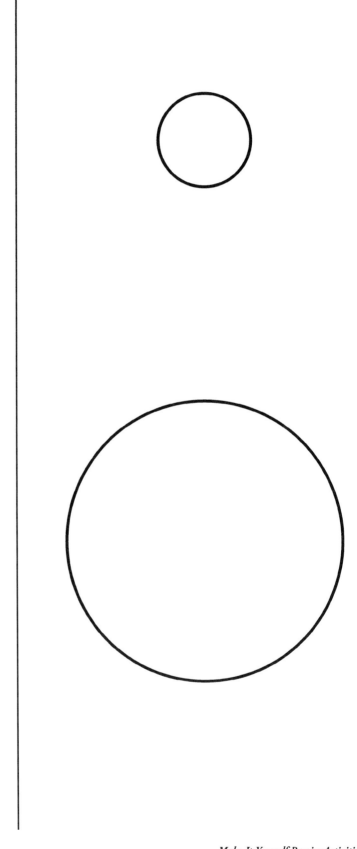

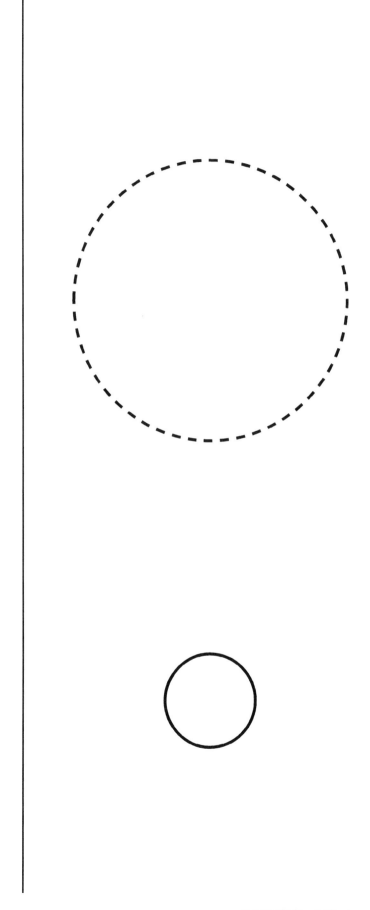

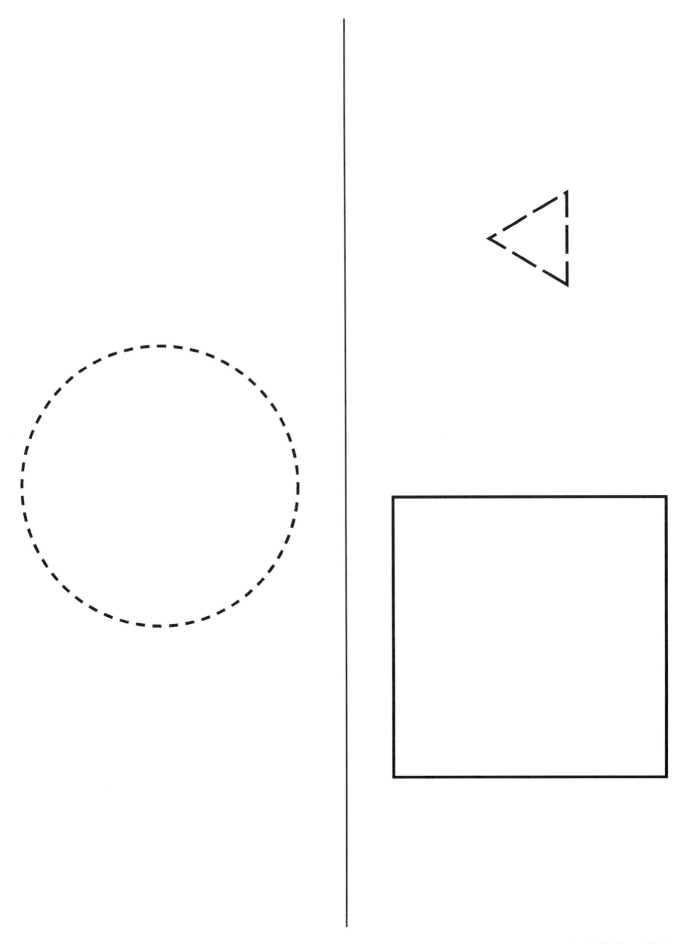

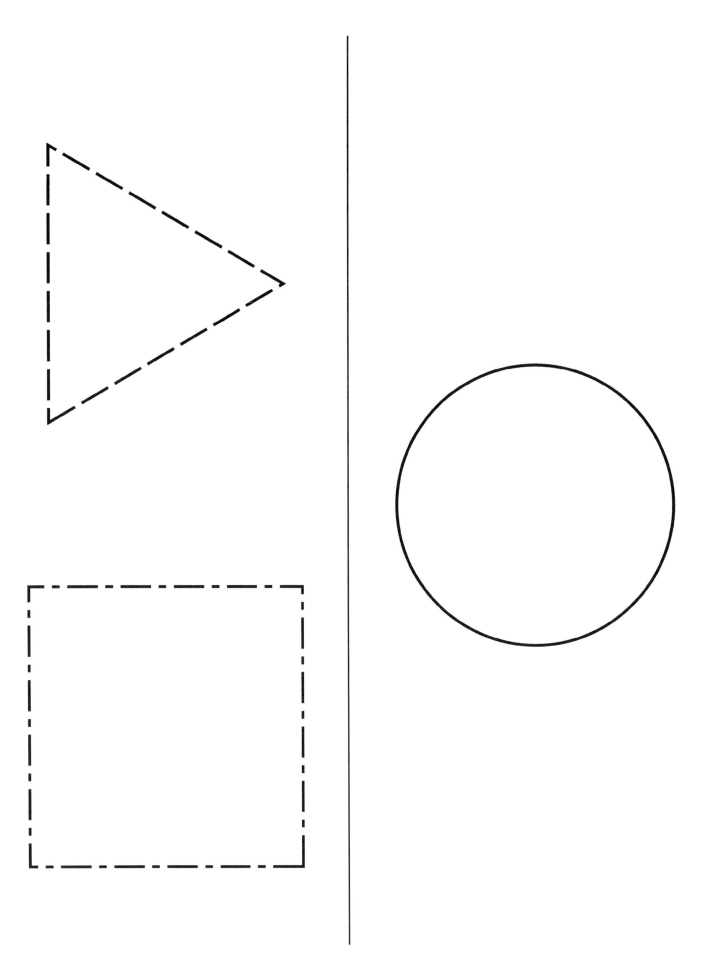

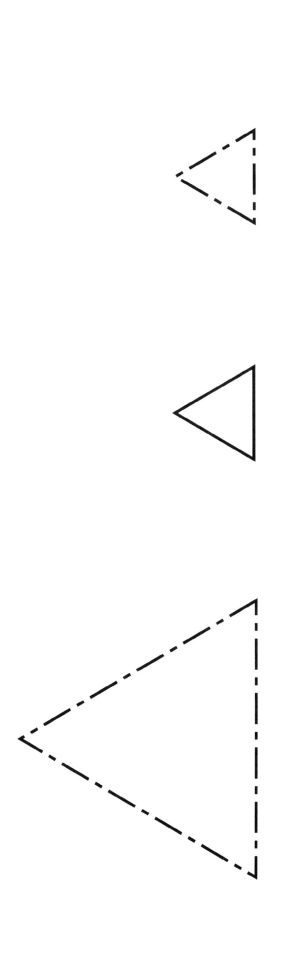

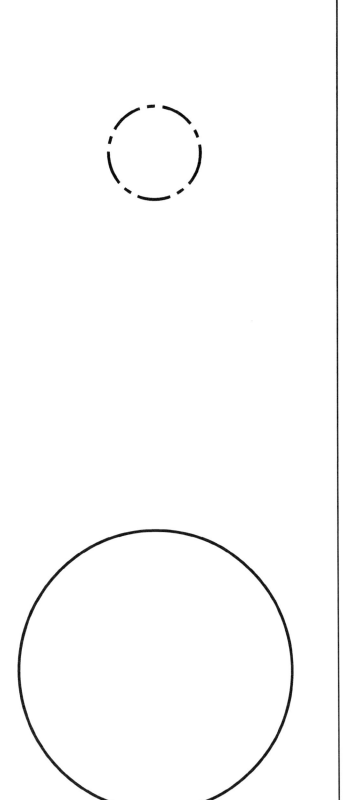

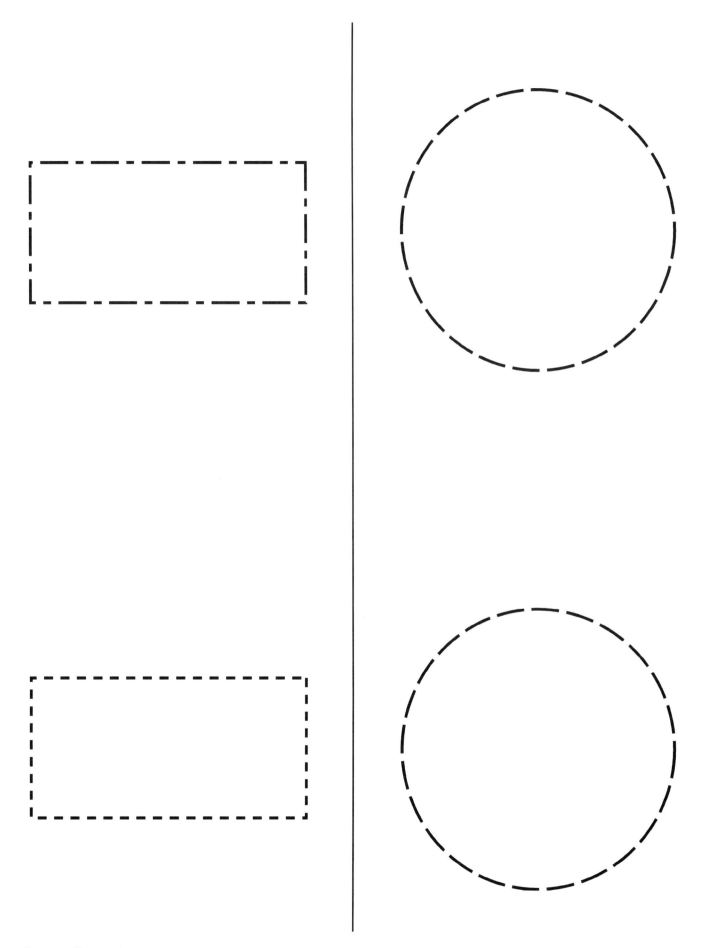

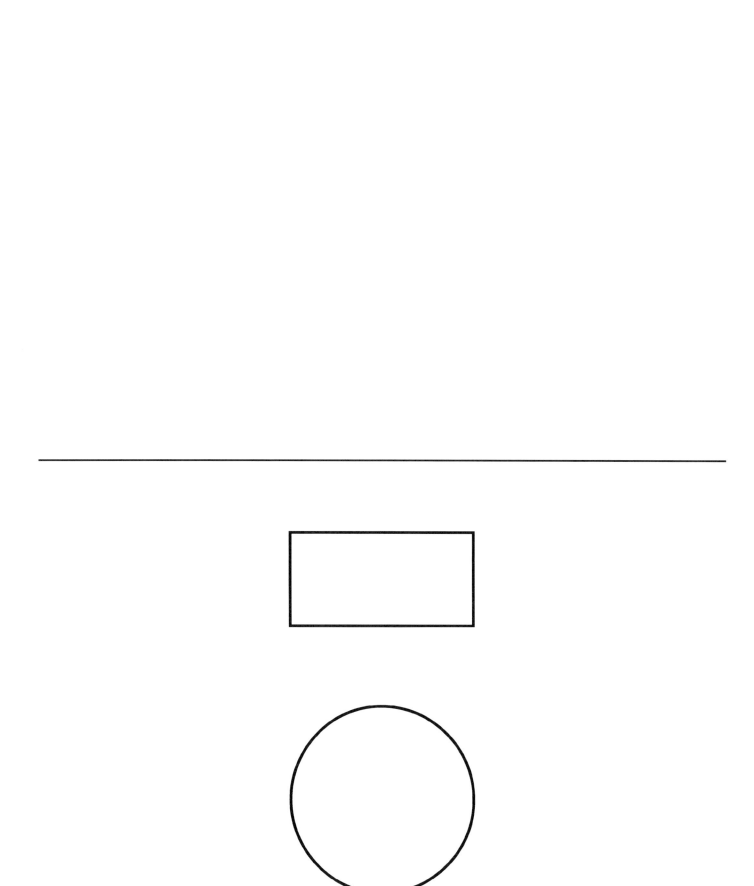

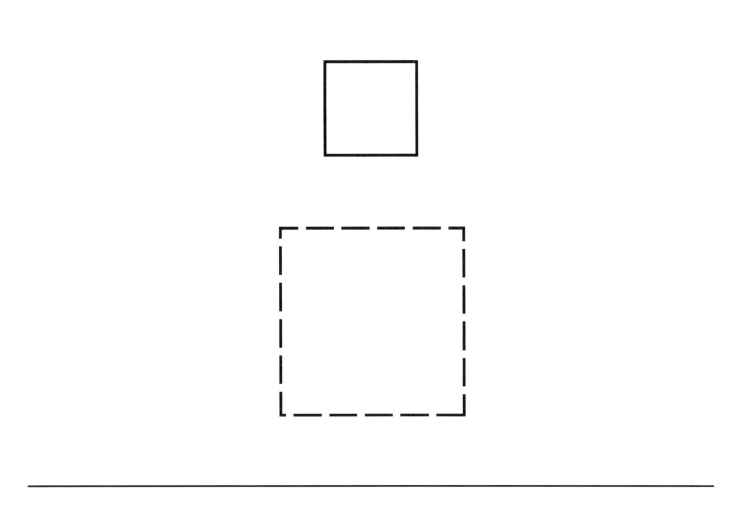

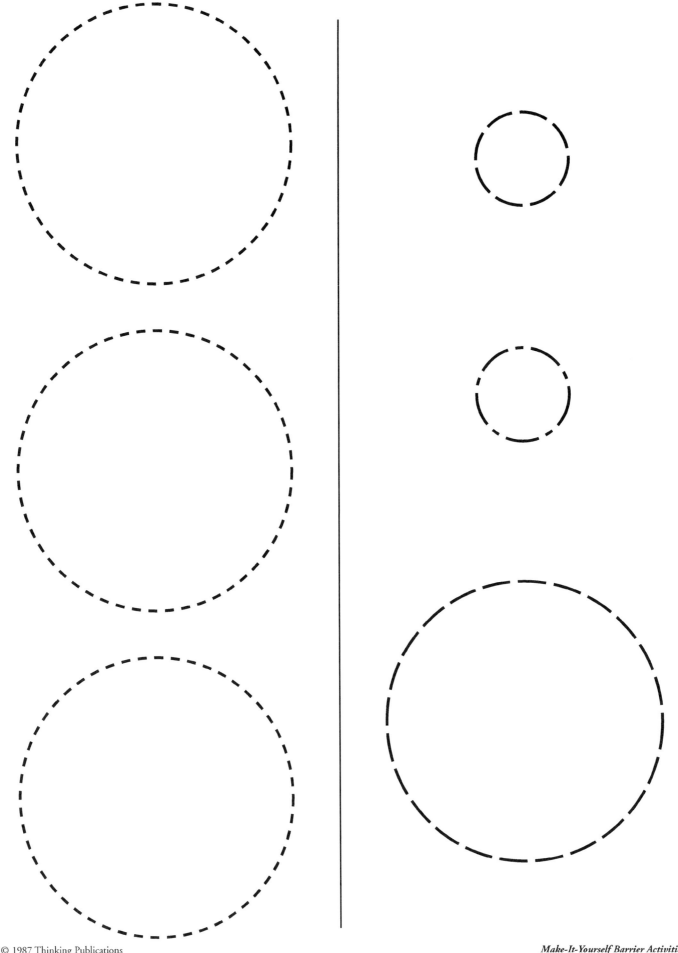

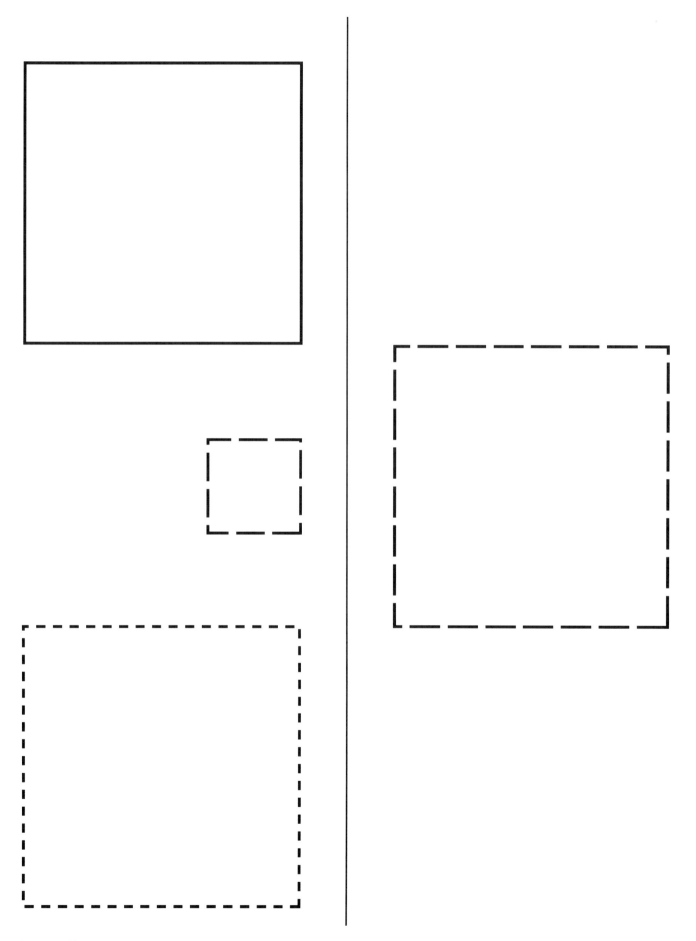

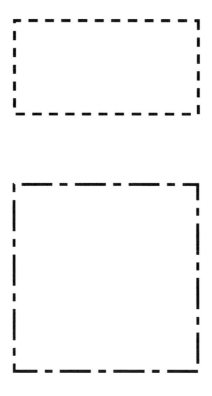

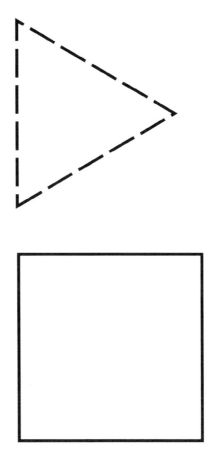

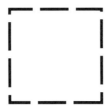

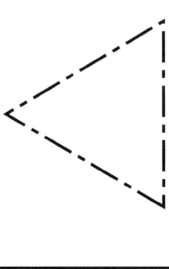

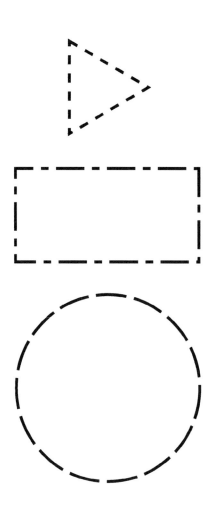

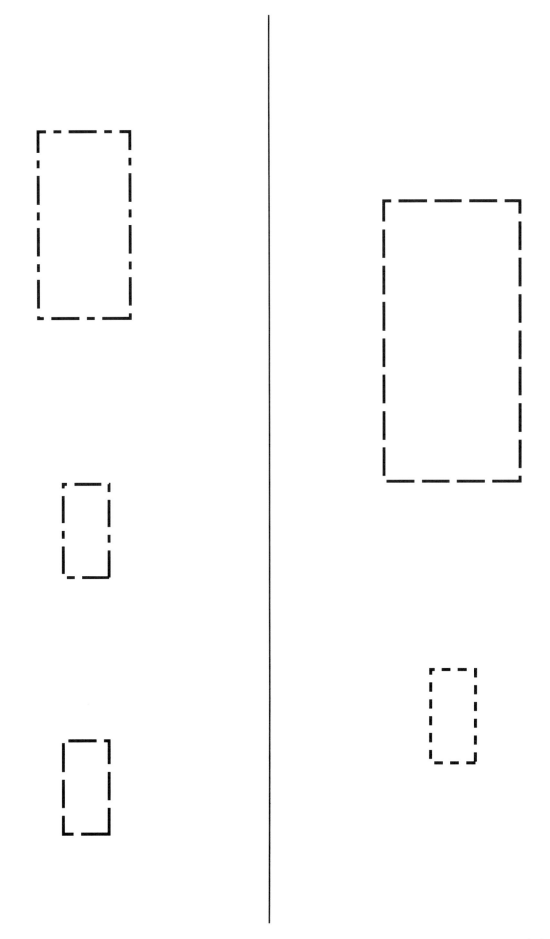

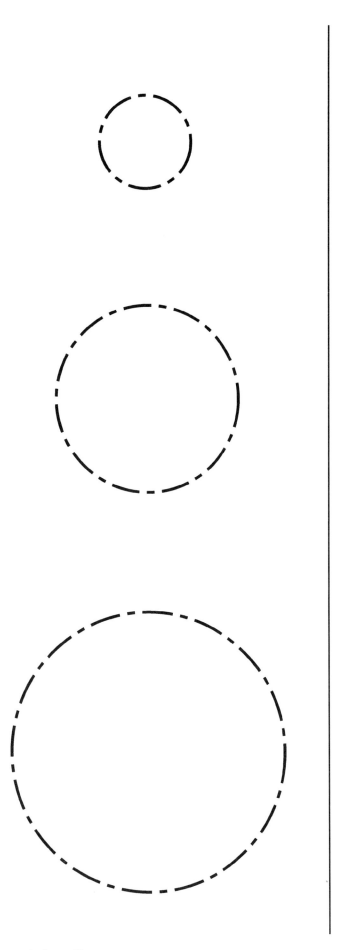

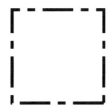

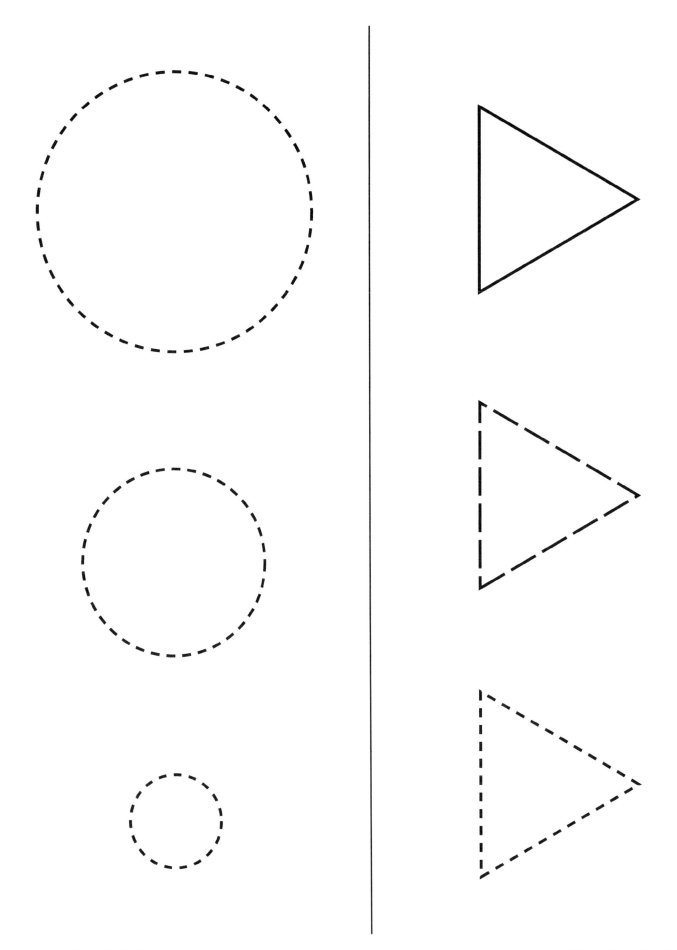

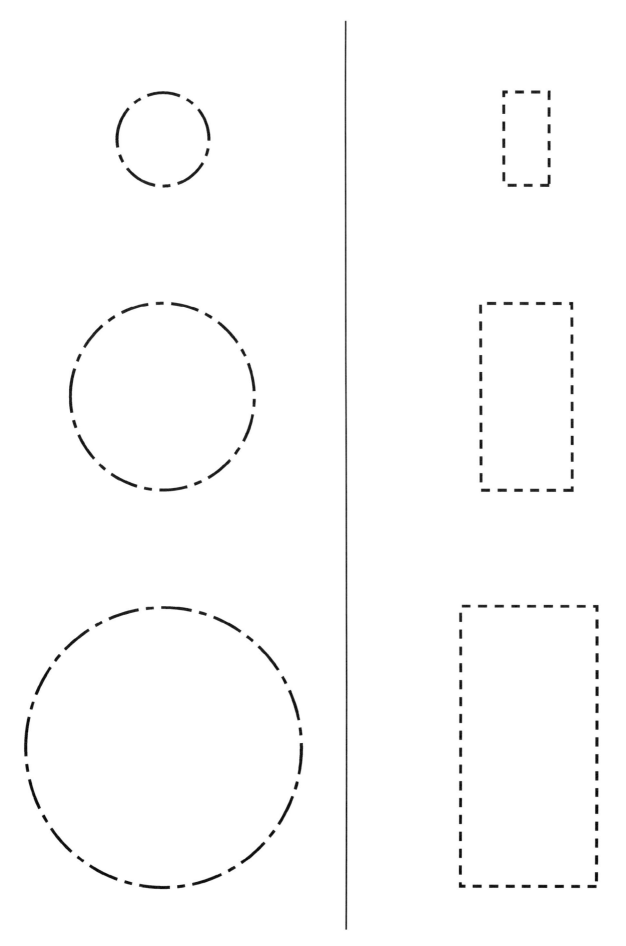

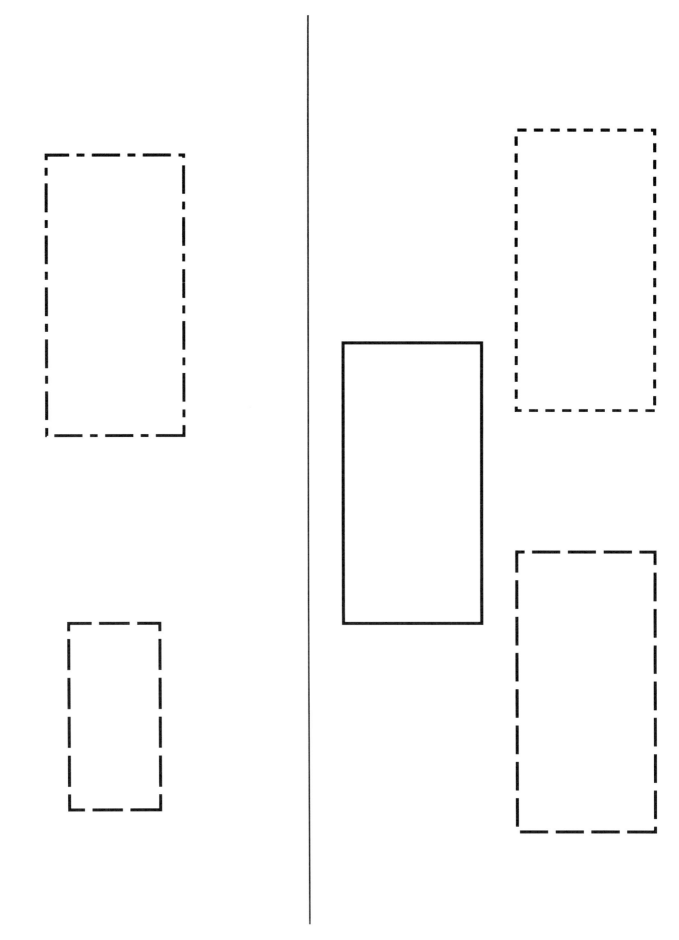

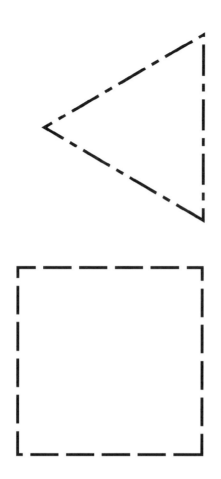
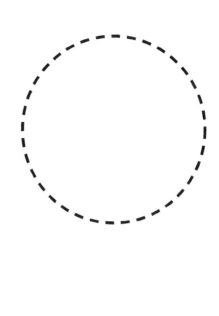

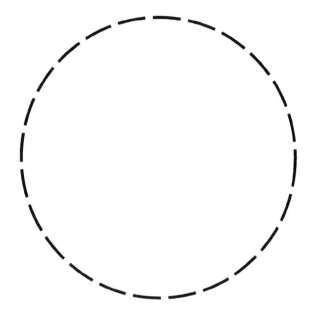

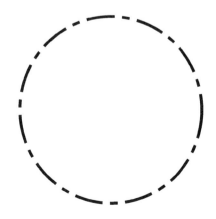

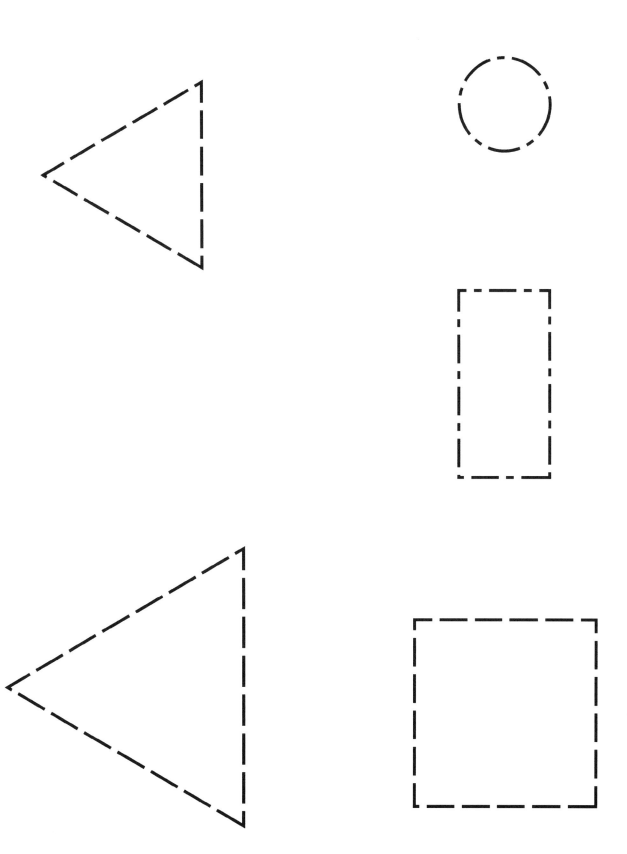

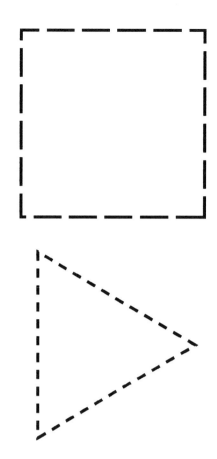
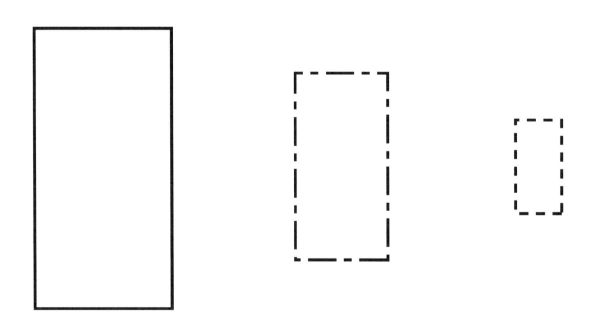

Part One Grids

Part Two Patterns

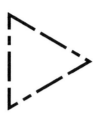

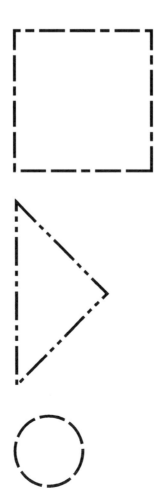

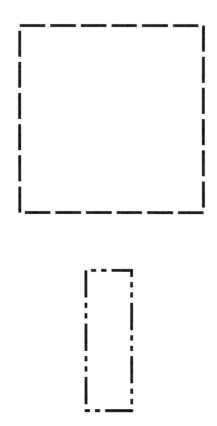

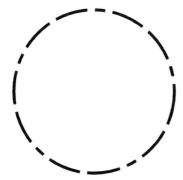

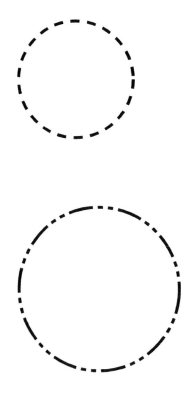

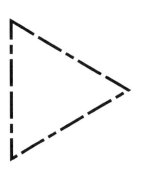

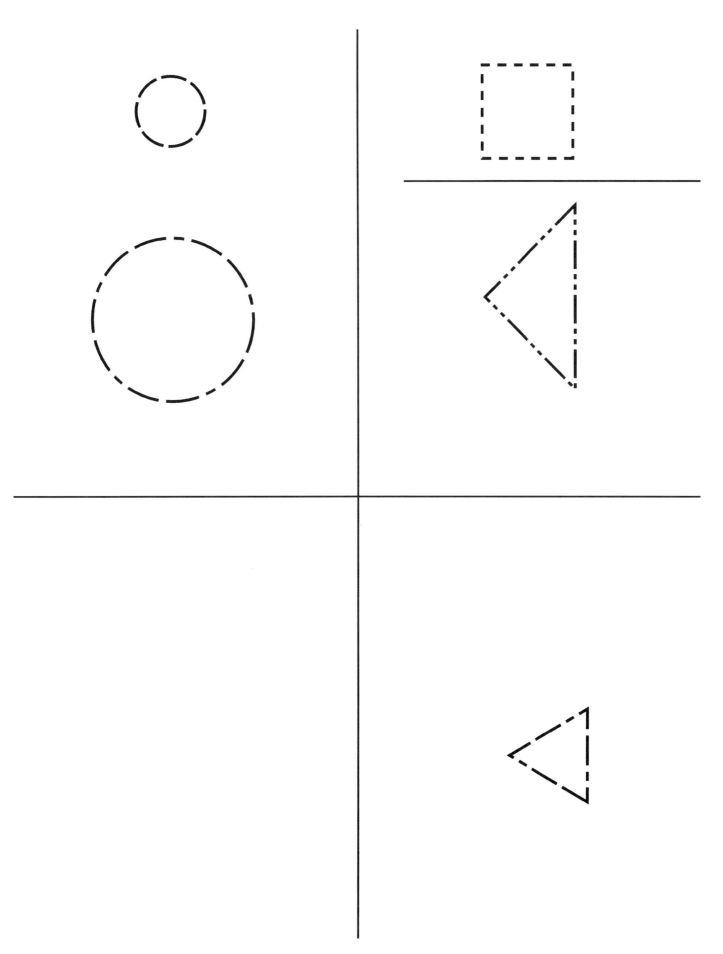

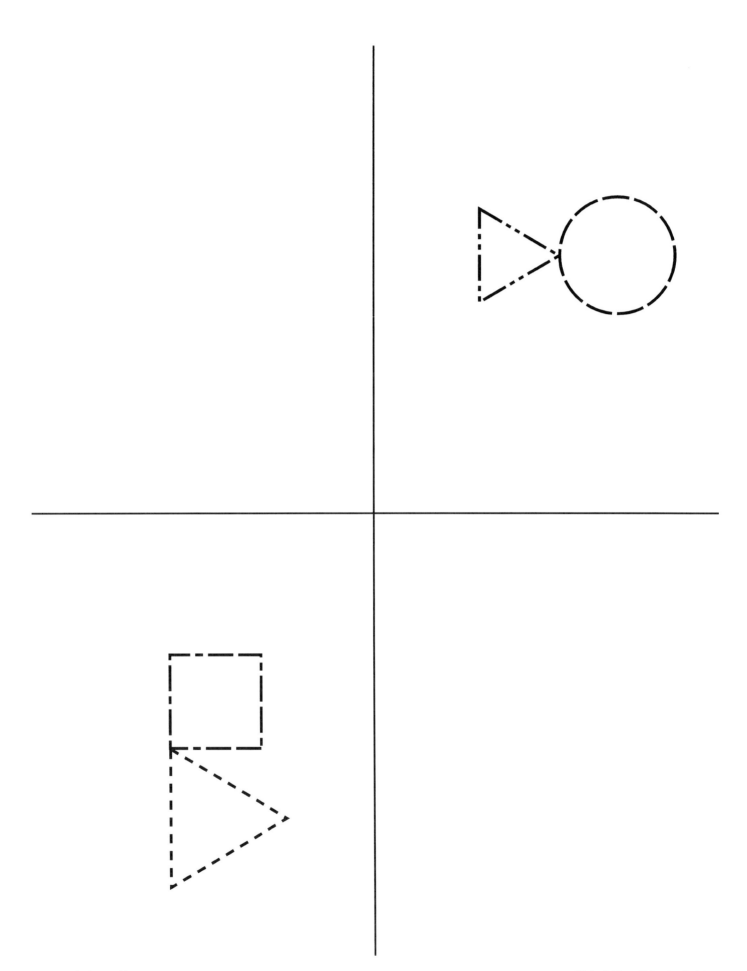

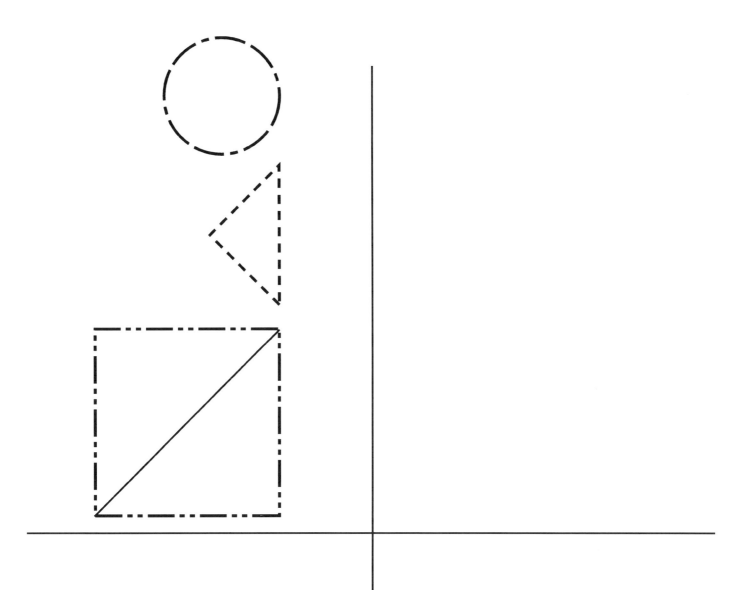

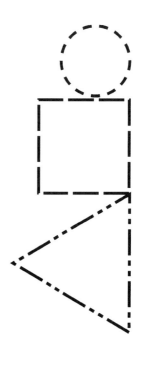

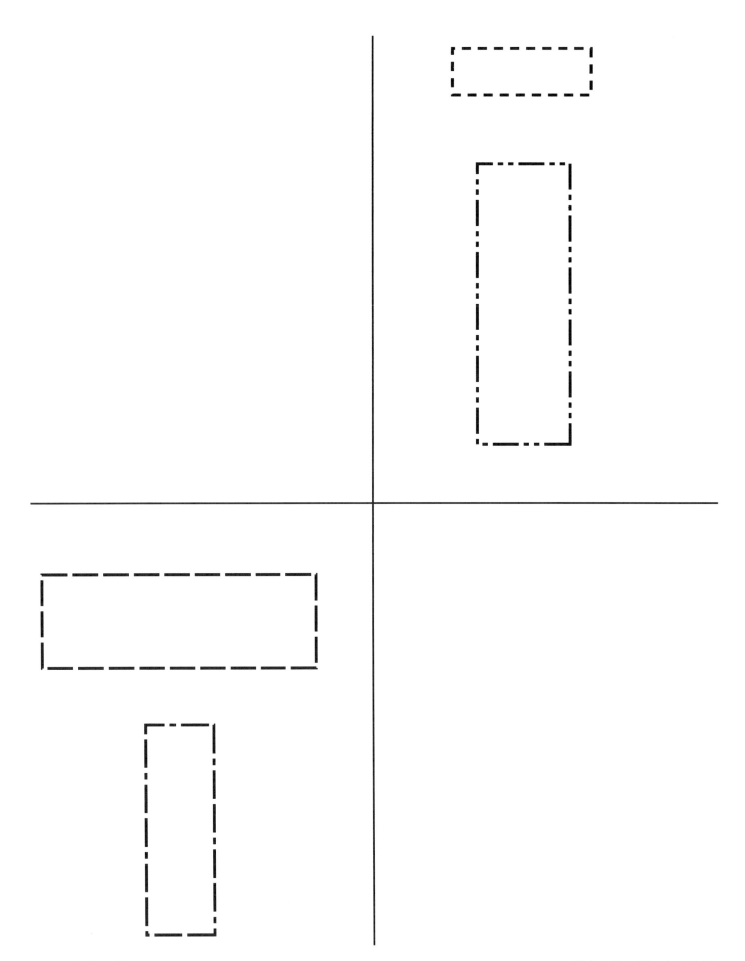

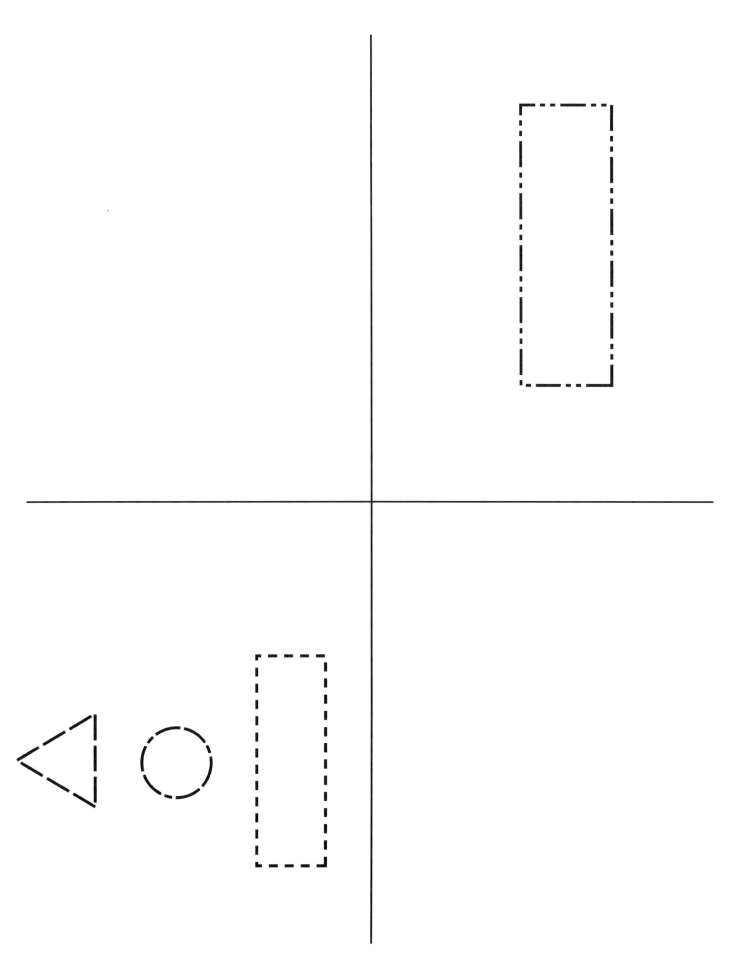

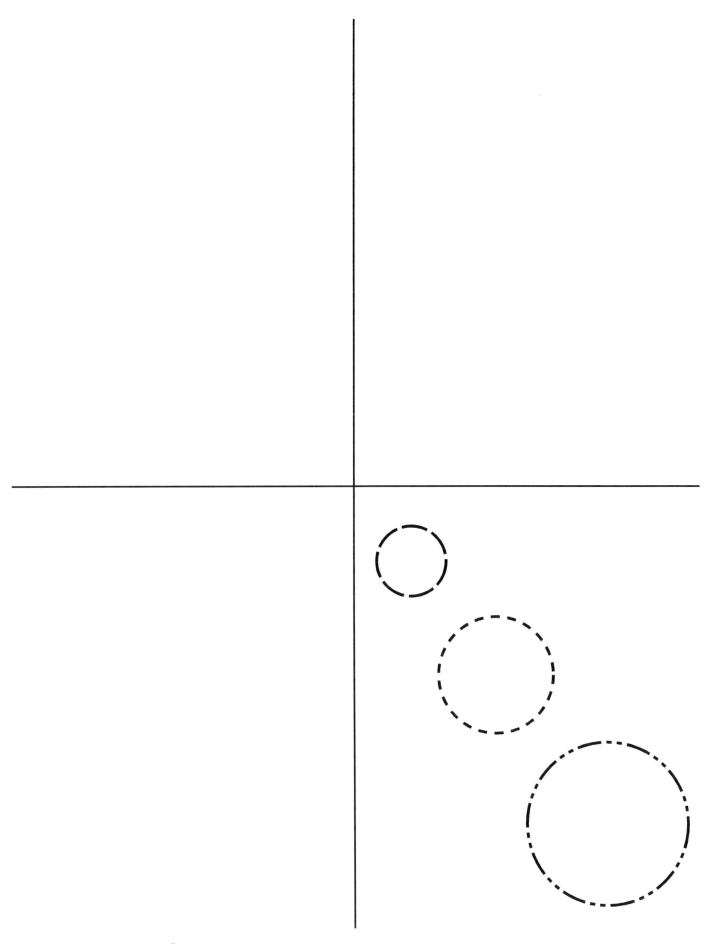

Make-It-Yourself Barrier Activities
(Part Two, Pattern 10)

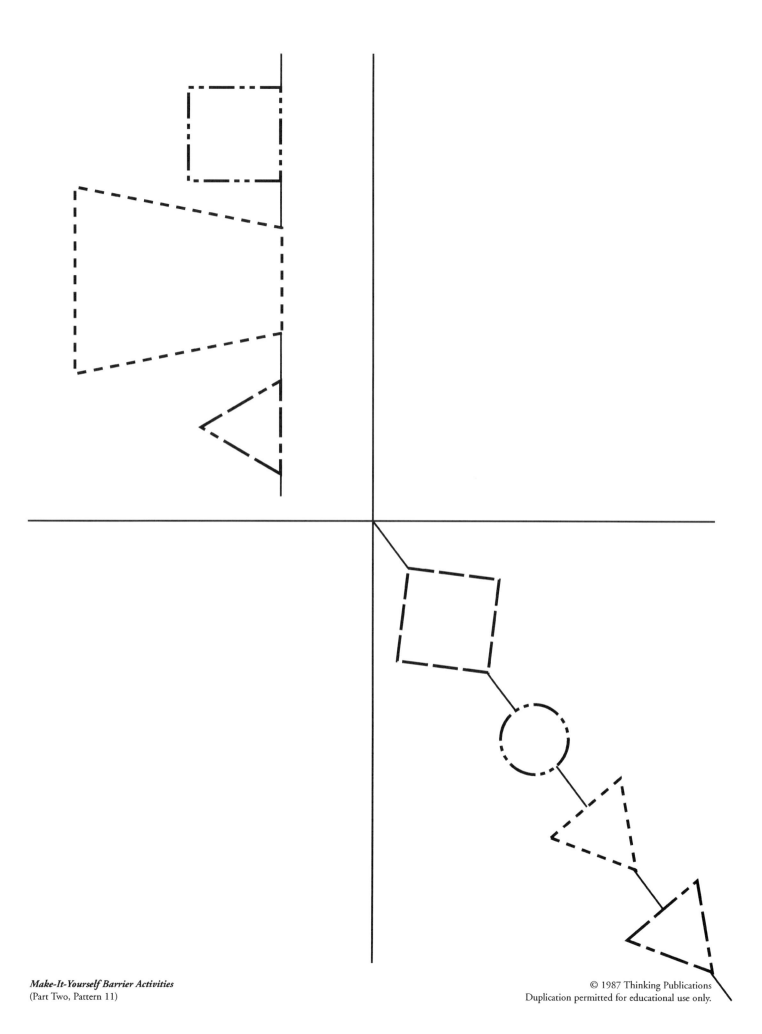

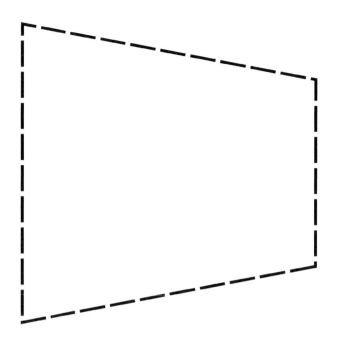

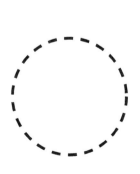

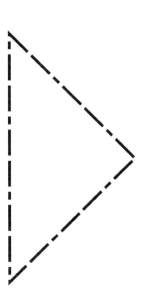

Make-It-Yourself Barrier Activities
(Part Two, Pattern 12)

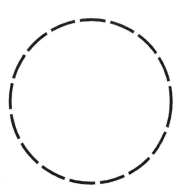

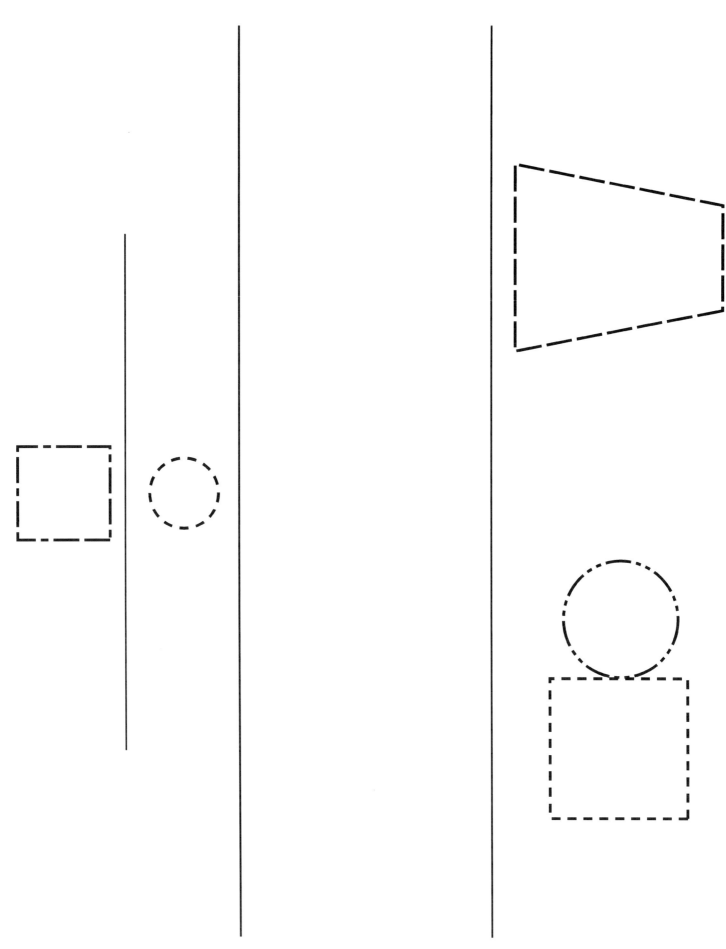

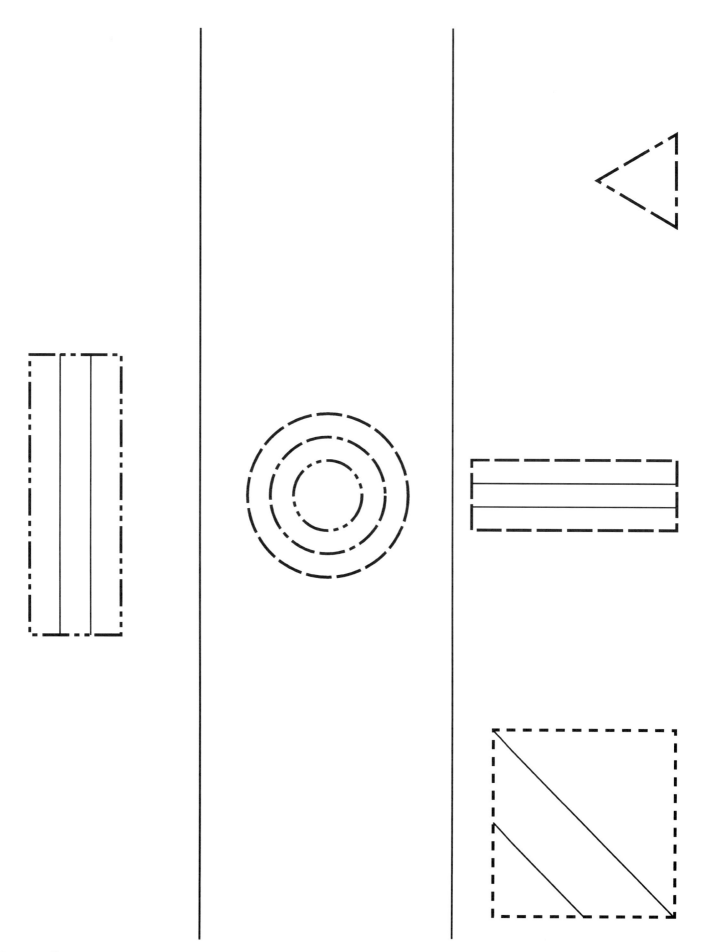

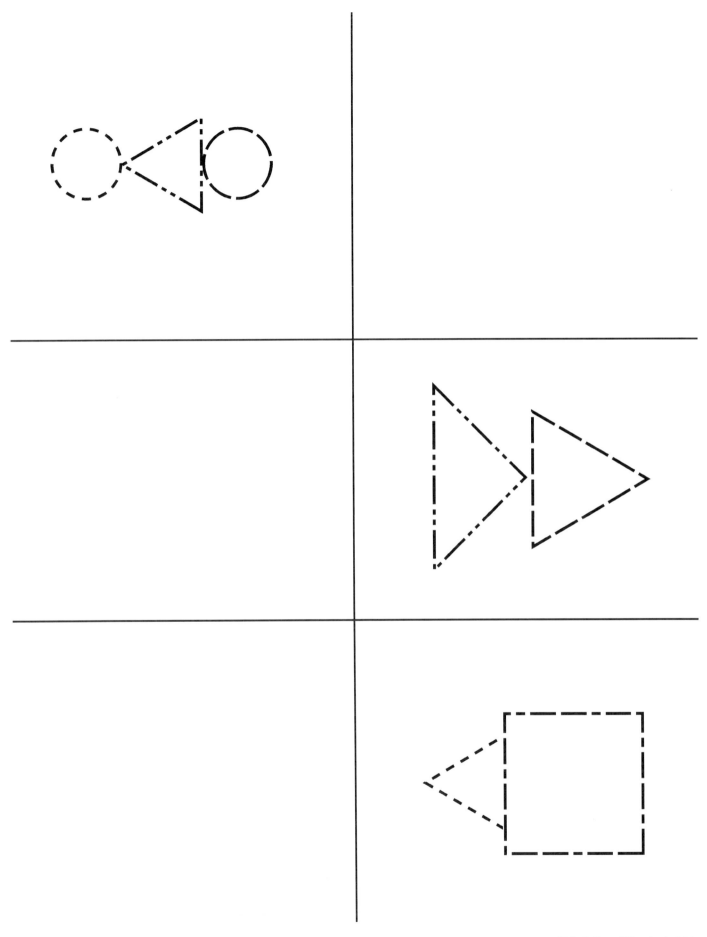

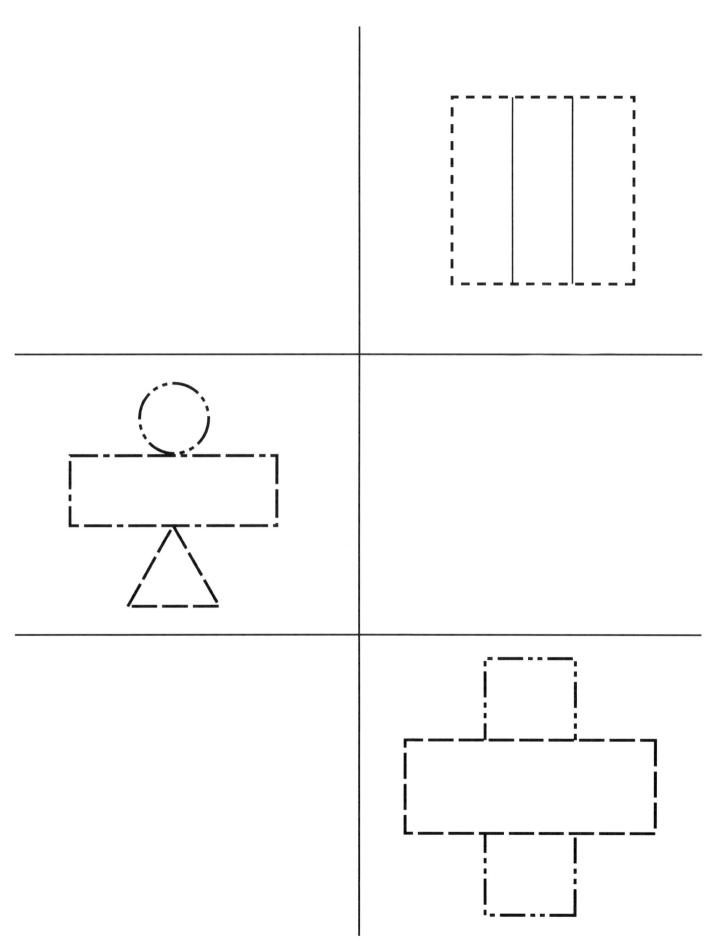

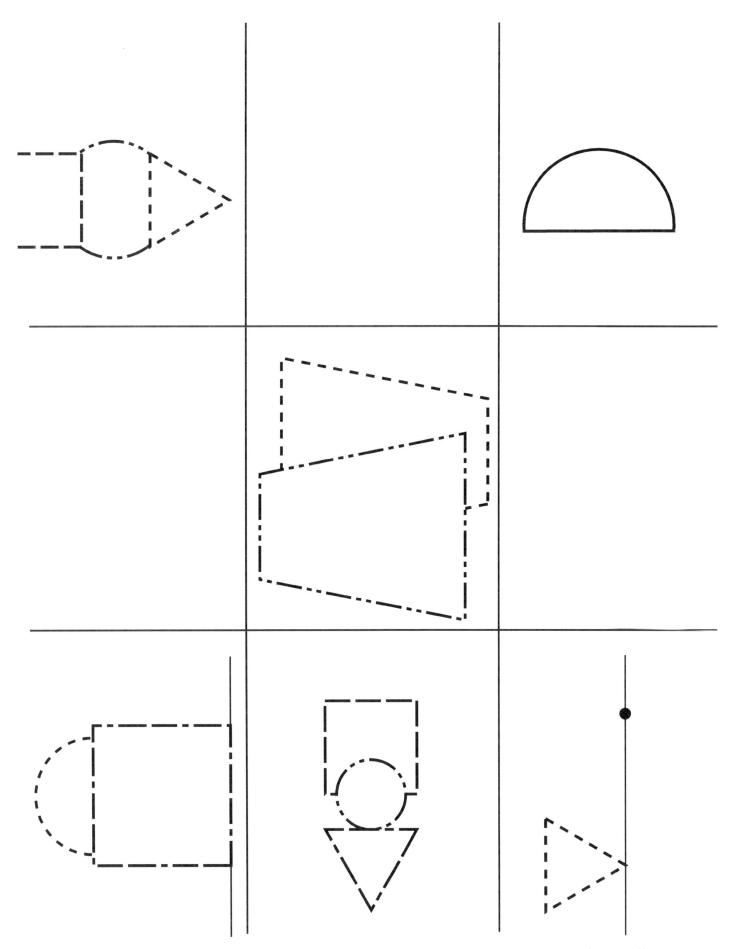

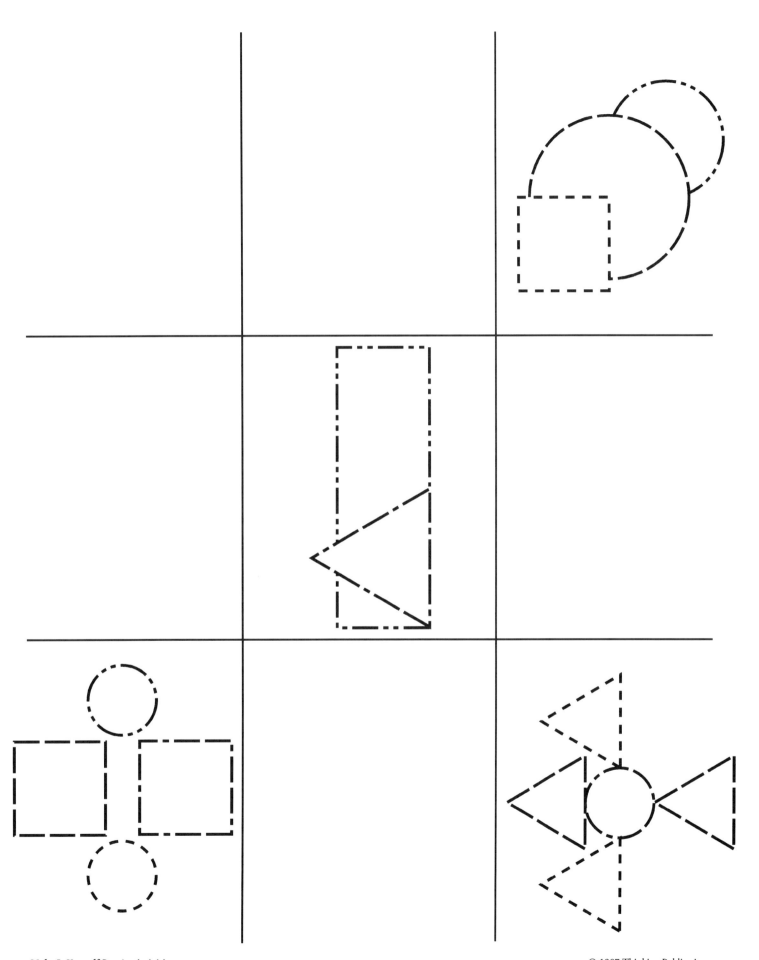

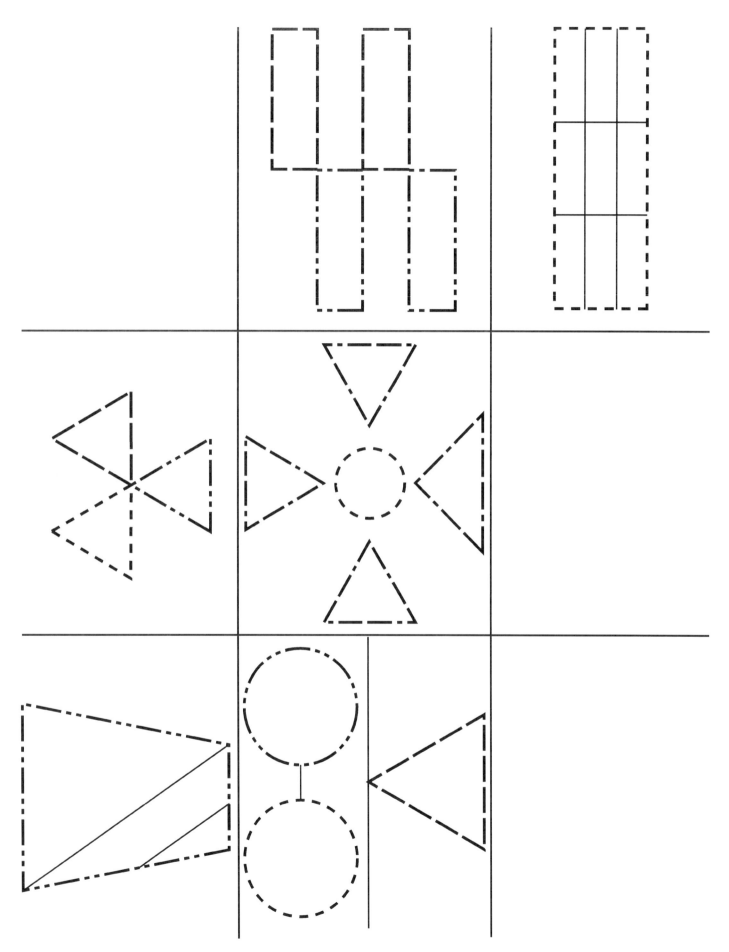

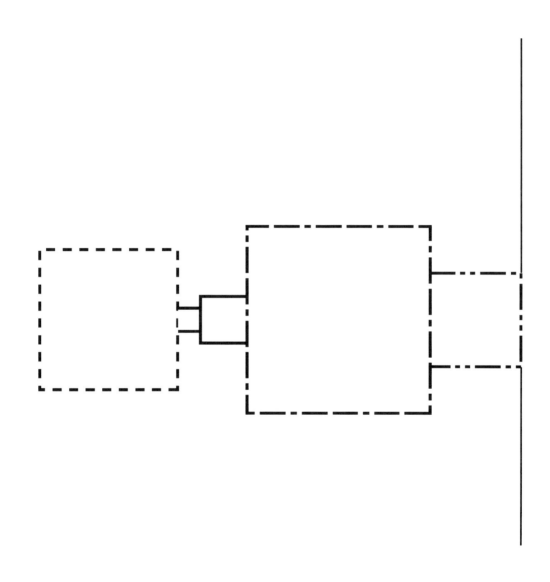

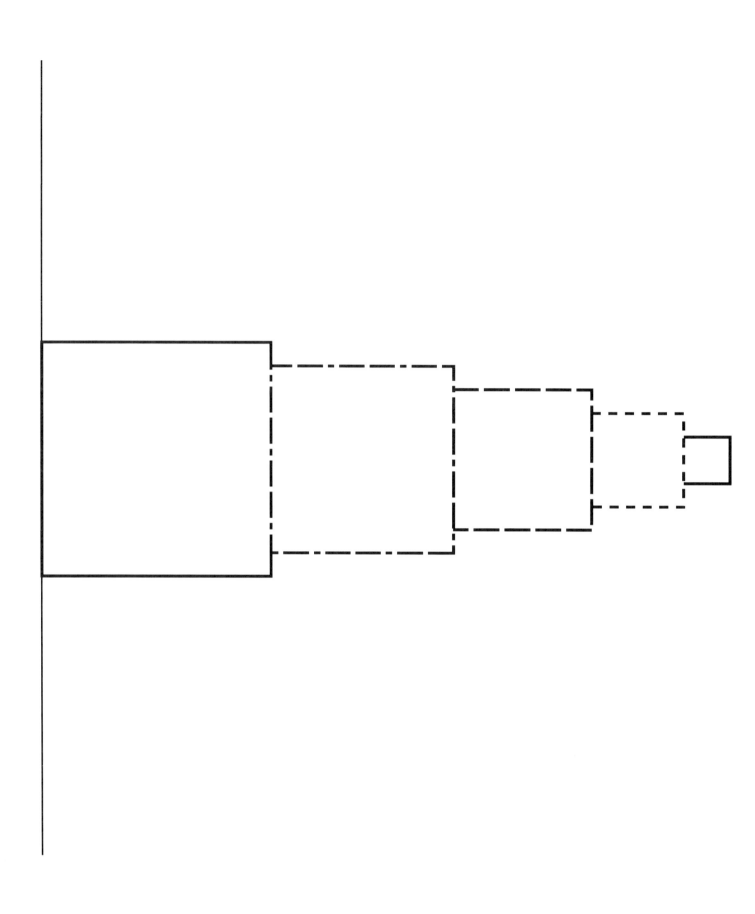

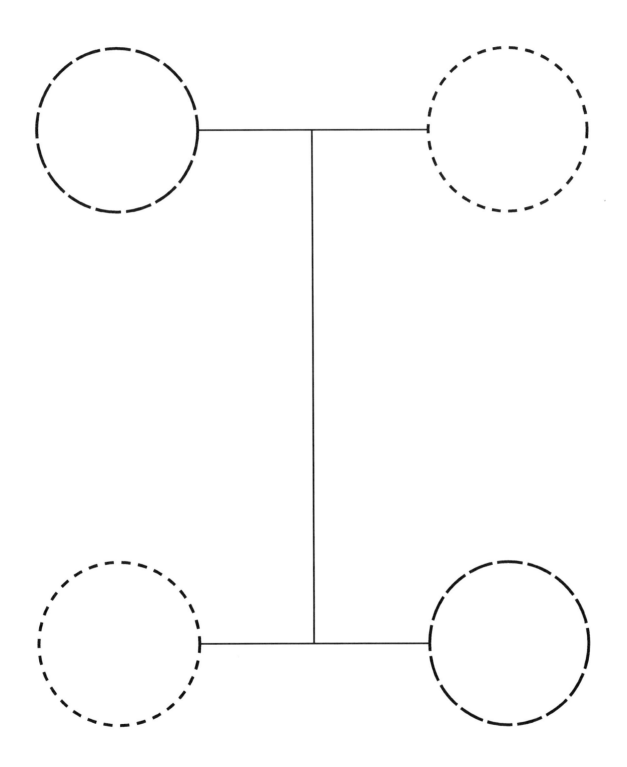

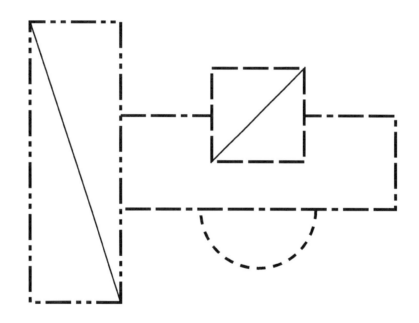

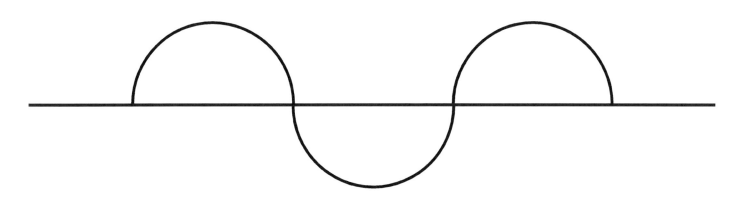

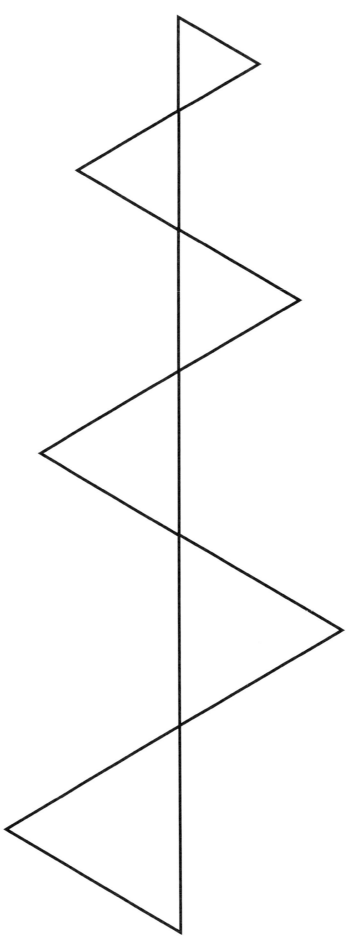

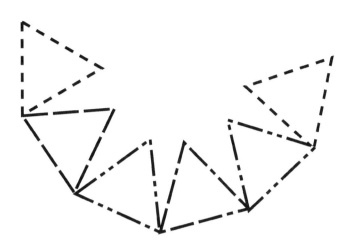

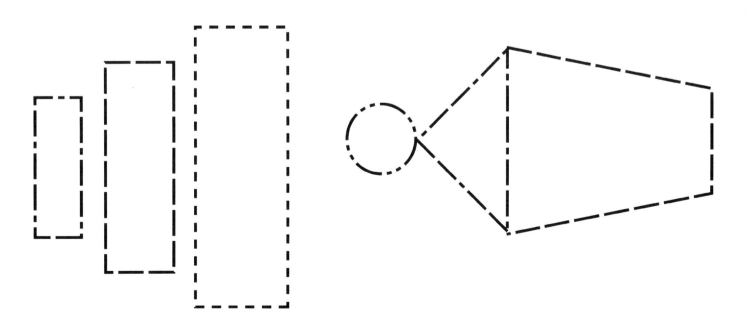

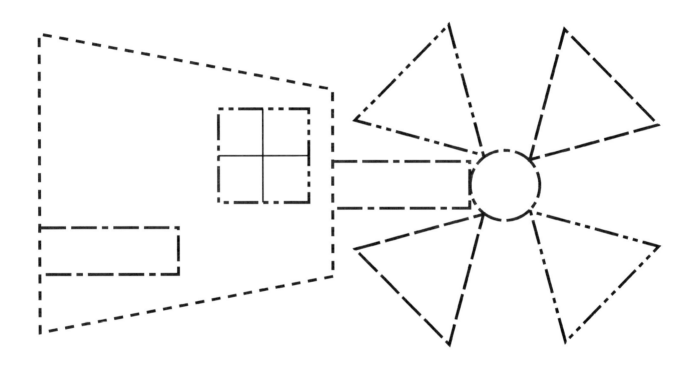

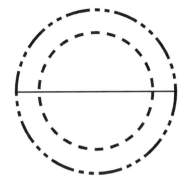

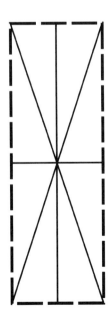

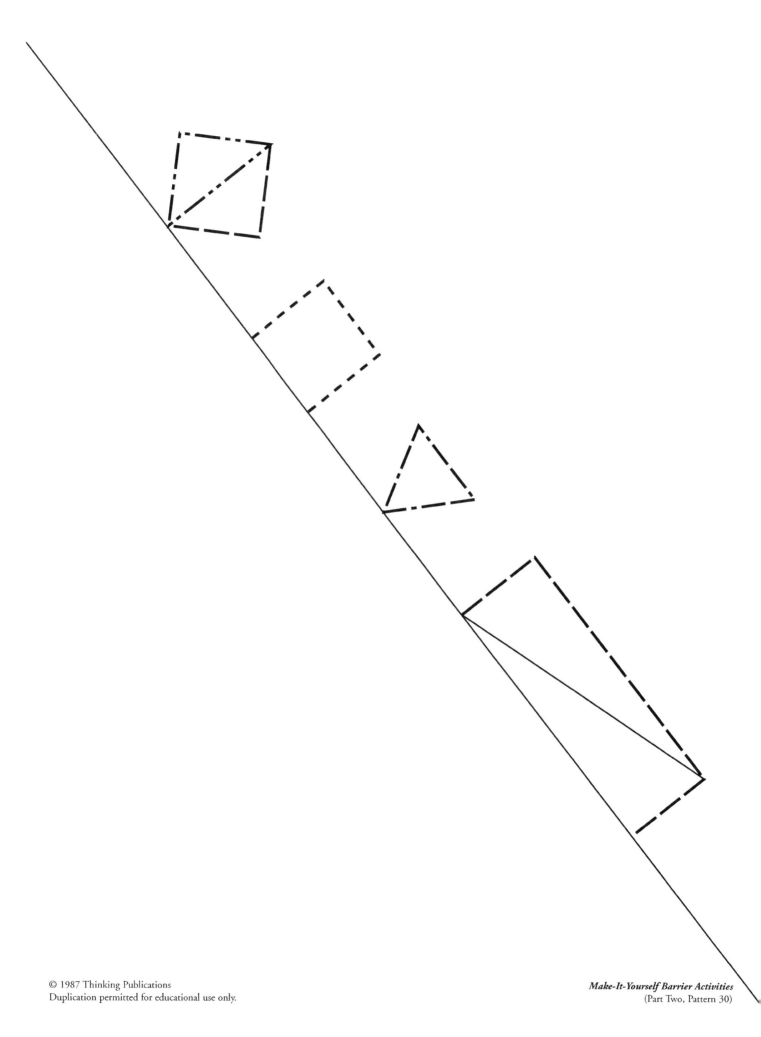

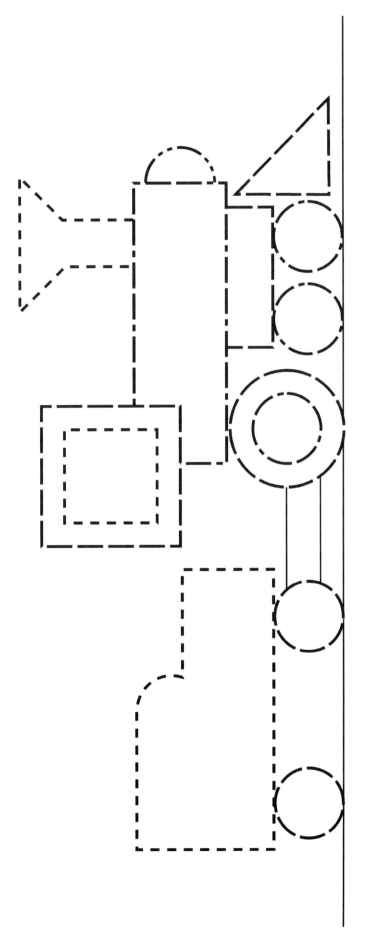

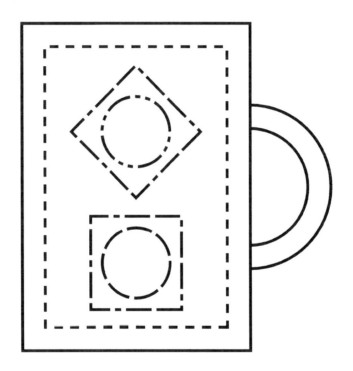

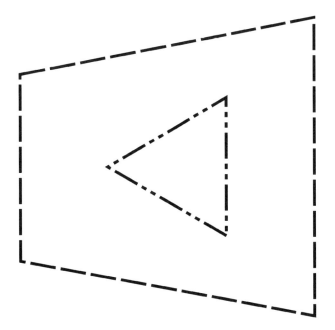

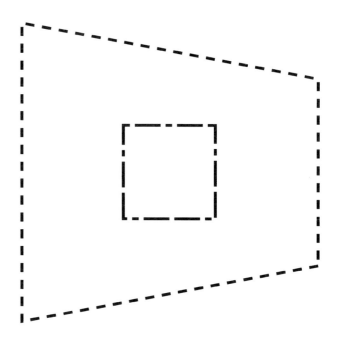

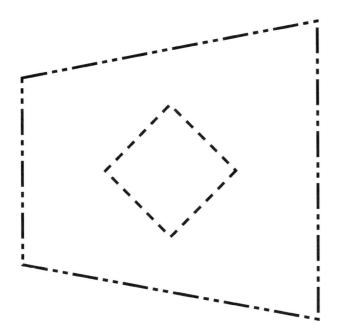

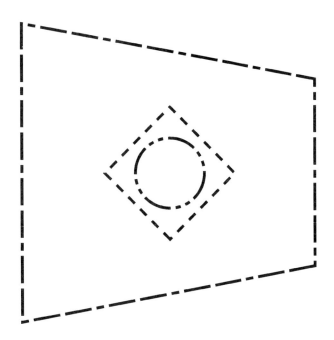

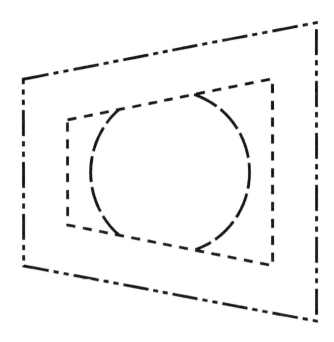

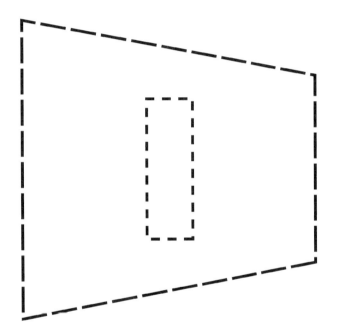 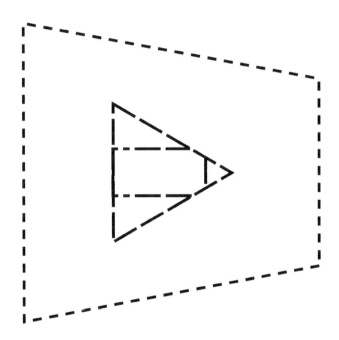

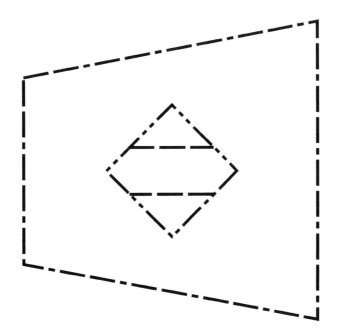

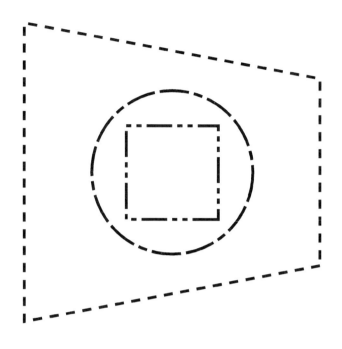

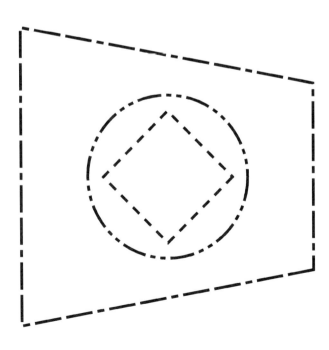

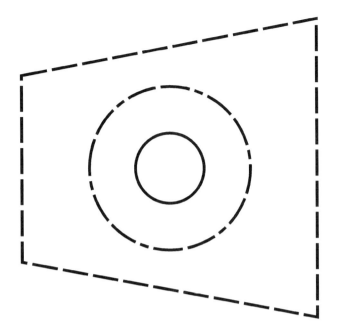

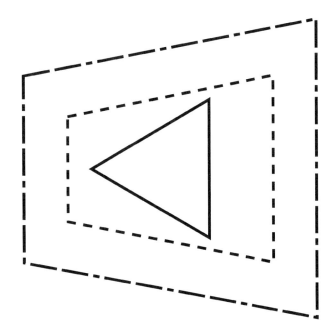

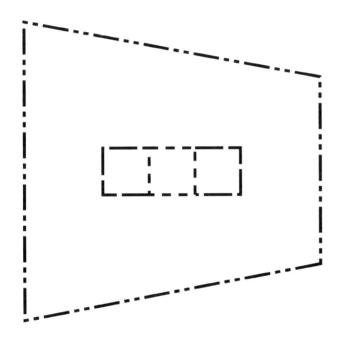

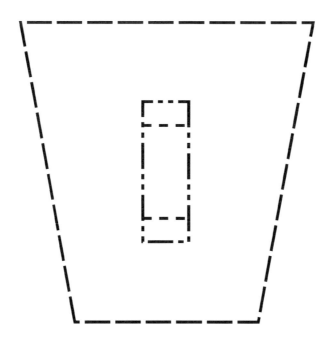

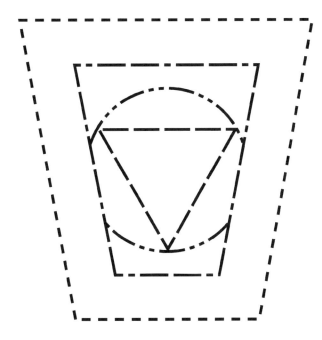

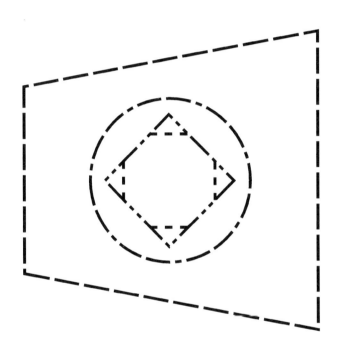

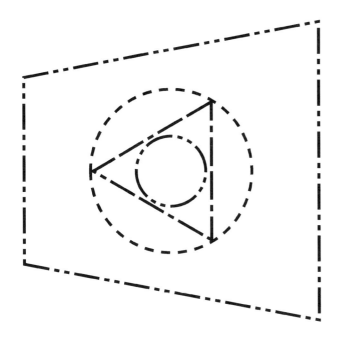

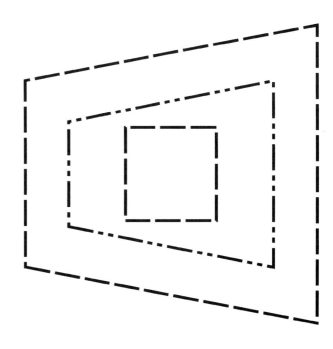

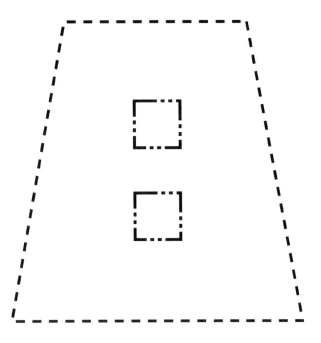

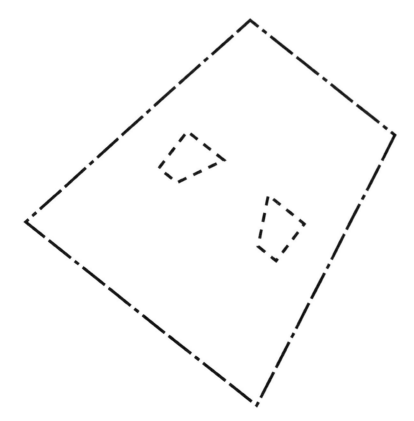

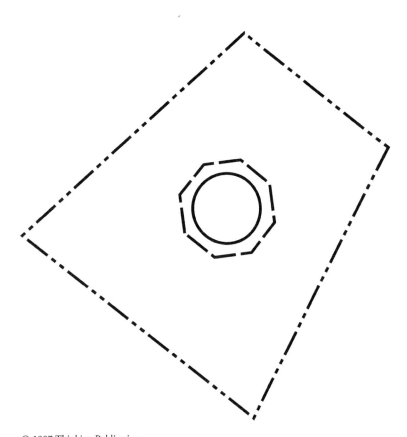

Part Two Grids

Geometric Form Masters

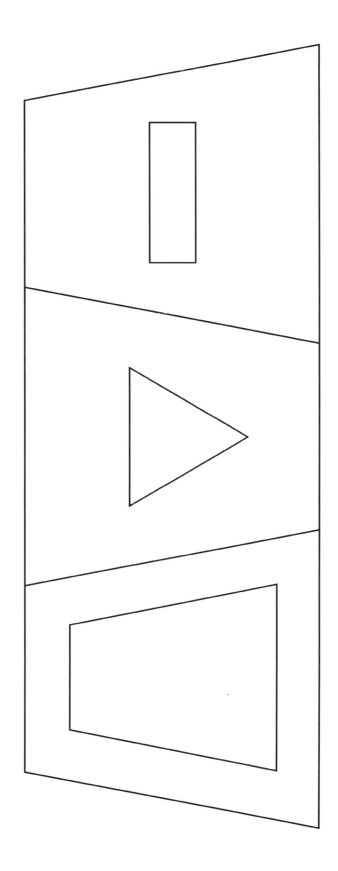

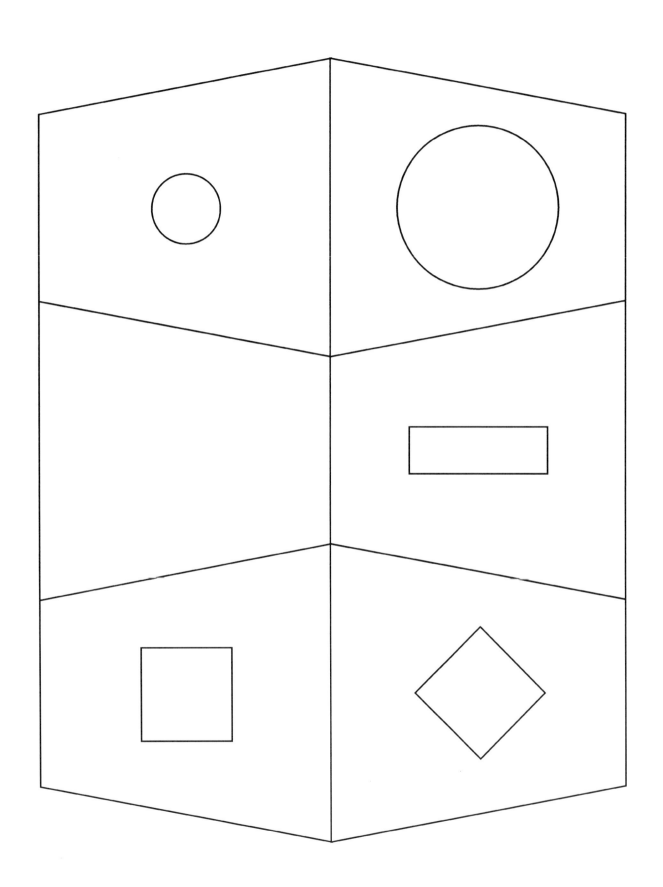